PENGUIN POPULAR POETRY

EIGHTEENTH CENTURY POETRY

SELECTED BY
PAUL DRIVER

PENGUIN BOOKS
A PENGUIN/GODFREY CAVE EDITION

PENGUIN BOOKS

Published by the Penguin Group
Penguin Books Ltd, 27 Wrights Lane, London w8 5tz, England
Penguin Books USA Inc., 375 Hudson Street, New York, New York 10014, USA
Penguin Books Australia Ltd, Ringwood, Victoria, Australia
Penguin Books Canada Ltd, 10 Alcorn Avenue, Toronto, Ontario, Canada m4v 3b2
Penguin Books (NZ) Ltd, 182–190 Wairau Road, Auckland 10, New Zealand

Penguin Books Ltd, Registered Offices: Harmondsworth, Middlesex, England

This edition first published 1995
Published in Penguin Popular Poetry 1996
1 3 5 7 9 10 8 6 4 2

Selection copyright © Paul Driver, 1995

Set in 9/11 pt Ehrhardt Monotype
Typeset by Datix International Limited, Bungay, Suffolk
Printed in England by Clays Ltd, St Ives plc

CONTENTS

iii

Epistle to Miss Blount, on her Leaving the Town, after the Coronation

As some fond virgin, whom her mother's care
Drags from the town to wholesome country air,
Just when she learns to roll a melting eye,
And hear a spark, yet think no danger nigh;
From the dear man unwilling she must sever,
Yet takes one kiss before she parts for ever:
Thus from the world fair Zephalinda flew,
Saw others happy, and with sighs withdrew;
Not that their pleasures caused her discontent,
She sighed not that they stayed, but that she went.

She went to plain-work, and to purling brooks,
Old-fashioned halls, dull aunts, and croaking rooks;
She went from op'ra, park, assembly, play,
To morning walks, and pray'rs three hours a day;
To pass her time 'twixt reading and bohea,
To muse, and spill her solitary tea,
Or o'er cold coffee trifle with the spoon,
Count the slow clock, and dine exact at noon;
Divert her eyes with pictures in the fire,
Hum half a tune, tell stories to the squire;
Up to her godly garret after sev'n,
There starve and pray, for that's the way to heav'n.

Some squire, perhaps, you take delight to rack,
Whose game is whisk, whose treat a toast in sack,
Who visits with a gun, presents you birds,
Then gives a smacking buss and cries, – No words!
Or with his hound comes hollowing from the stable,
Makes love with nods, and knees beneath a table;
Whose laughs are hearty, though his jests are coarse,
And loves you best of all things – but his horse.

In some fair evening, on your elbow laid,
You dream of triumphs in the rural shade;
In pensive thought recall the fancied scene,
See coronations rise on ev'ry green;

Before you pass th' imaginary sights
Of lords, and earls, and dukes, and gartered knights,
While the spread fan o'ershades your closing eyes;
Then give one flirt, and all the vision flies.
Thus vanish sceptres, coronets, and balls,
And leave you in lone woods, or empty walls.
  So when your slave, at some dear, idle time
(Not plagued with head-aches, or the want of rhyme),
Stands in the streets, abstracted from the crew,
And while he seems to study, thinks of you:
Just when his fancy points your sprightly eyes,
Or sees the blush of soft Parthenia rise,
Gay pats my shoulder, and you vanish quite;
Streets, chairs, and coxcombs rush upon my sight;
Vexed to be still in town, I knit my brow,
Look sour, and hum a tune – as you may now.

ALEXANDER POPE

To Their Excellencies the Lords Justices of Ireland.
The Humble Petition of Frances Harris, Who Must
Starve and Die a Maid If It Miscarries

Humbly showeth:

THAT I went to warm myself in Lady Betty's chamber, because I was cold,

And I had in a purse, seven pound, four shillings and sixpence, besides farthings, in money, and gold;

So because I had been buying things for my Lady last night,

I was resolved to tell my money, to see if it was right.

Now you must know, because my trunk has a very bad lock,

Therefore all the money I have, which, God knows, is a very small stock,

I keep in a pocket tied about my middle, next my smock.

So when I went to put up my purse, as God would have it, my smock was unripped,

And, instead of putting it into my pocket, down it slipped:

2

Then the bell rung, and I went down to put my Lady to bed,

And, God knows, I thought my money was as safe as my maidenhead.

So when I came up again, I found my pocket feel very light,

But when I searched, and missed my purse, Lord! I thought I should have sunk outright.

'Lord! Madam,' says Mary, 'how d'ye do?' – 'Indeed,' said I, 'never worse;

But pray, Mary, can you tell what I have done with my purse?'

'Lord help me,' said Mary, 'I never stirred out of this place!'

'Nay,' said I, 'I had it in Lady Betty's chamber, that's a plain case.'

So Mary got me to bed, and covered me up warm,

However, she stole away my garters, that I might do myself no harm.

So I tumbled and tossed all night, as you may very well think,

But hardly ever set my eyes together, or slept a wink.

So I was a-dreamed, methought, that we went and searched the folks round,

And in a corner of Mrs Dukes' box, tied in a rag, the money was found.

So next morning we told Whittle, and he fell a-swearing;

Then my Dame Wadgar came, and she, you know, is thick of hearing;

'Dame,' said I, as loud as I could bawl, 'do you know what a loss I have had?'

'Nay,' said she, 'my Lord Collway's folks are all very sad,

For my Lord Dromedary comes a Tuesday without fail';

'Pugh!' said I, 'but that's not the business that I ail.'

Says Cary, says he, 'I have been a servant this five and twenty years, come spring,

And in all the places I lived, I never heard of such a thing.'

'Yes,' says the steward, 'I remember when I was at my Lady Shrewsbury's,

Such a thing as this happened, just about the time of gooseberries.'

So I went to the party suspected, and I found her full of grief;

(Now you must know, of all things in the world, I hate a thief).

However, I was resolved to bring the discourse slyly about.

'Mrs Dukes,' said I, 'here's an ugly accident has happened out;

'Tis not that I value the money three skips of a louse;

But the thing I stand upon is the credit of the House;

'Tis true, seven pound, four shillings, and sixpence, makes a great hole in my wages,

Besides, as they say, service is no inheritance in these ages.
Now, Mrs Dukes, you know, and everybody understands,
That though 'tis hard to judge, yet money can't go without hands.'
'The devil take me,' said she (blessing herself), 'if ever I saw't!'
So she roared like a Bedlam, as though I had called her all to naught;
So you know, what could I say to her any more?
I e'en left her, and came away as wise as I was before.
Well: but then they would have had me gone to the cunning man;
'No,' said I, ''tis the same thing, the chaplain will be here anon.'
So the chaplain came in. Now the servants say he is my sweetheart,
Because he's always in my chamber, and I always take his part;
So, as the devil would have it, before I was aware, out I blundered,
'Parson,' said I, 'can you cast a nativity, when a body's plundered?'
(Now you must know, he hates to be called parson, like the devil.)
'Truly,' says he, 'Mrs Nab, it might become you to be more civil;
If your money be gone, as a learned divine says, d'ye see,
You are no text for my handling, so take that from me;
I was never taken for a conjurer before, I'd have you to know.'
'Lord,' said I, 'don't be angry, I'm sure I never thought you so;
You know I honour the cloth, I design to be a parson's wife,
I never took one in your coat for a conjurer in all my life.'
With that, he twisted his girdle at me like a rope, as who should say,
'Now you may go hang yourself for me', and so went away.
Well, I thought I should have swooned: 'Lord,' said I, 'what shall I do?
I have lost my money, and I shall lose my true-love too.'
Then my Lord called me; 'Harry,' said my Lord, 'don't cry,
I'll give something towards thy loss'; and says my Lady, 'so will I'.
'Oh but', said I, 'what if after all the chaplain won't come to?'
For that, he said (an't please your Excellencies) I must petition you.

The premises tenderly considered, I desire your Excellencies'
    protection,
And that I may have a share in next Sunday's collection:
And over and above, that I may have your Excellencies' letter
With an order for the chaplain aforesaid, or instead of him, a better;
And then your poor petitioner, both night and day,
Or the chaplain (for 'tis his trade) as in duty bound, shall ever pray.

JONATHAN SWIFT

4

An Ode

The merchant, to secure his treasure,
    Conveys it in a borrowed name:
Euphelia serves to grace my measure,
    But Cloe is my real flame.

My softest verse, my darling lyre,
    Upon Euphelia's toilet lay,
When Cloe noted her desire
    That I should sing, that I should play.

My lyre I tune, my voice I raise,
    But with my numbers mix my sighs:
And whilst I sing Euphelia's praise,
    I fix my soul on Cloe's eyes.

Fair Cloe blushed, Euphelia frowned;
    I sung and gazed, I played and trembled;
And Venus to the Loves around
    Remarked how ill we all dissembled.

MATTHEW PRIOR

A Better Answer to Cloe Jealous

Dear Cloe, how blubbered is that pretty face,
    Thy cheek all on fire, and thy hair all uncurled:
Pr'ythee quit this caprice; and (as old Falstaff says)
    Let us e'en talk a little like folks of this world.

How canst thou presume thou hast leave to destroy
    The beauties, which Venus but lent to thy keeping?
Those looks were designed to inspire love and joy:
    More ord'nary eyes may serve people for weeping.

To be vexed at a trifle or two that I writ,
    Your judgement at once and my passion you wrong:

You take that for fact, which will scarce be found wit:
    Od's life! must one swear to the truth of a song?

What I speak, my fair Cloe, and what I write, shows
    The diff'rence there is betwixt nature and art:
I court others in verse, but I love thee in prose:
    And they have my whimsies, but thou hast my heart.

The god of us verse-men (you know, child) the sun,
    How after his journeys he sets up his rest:
If at morning o'er earth 'tis his fancy to run,
    At night he reclines on his Thetis's breast.

So when I am wearied with wand'ring all day,
    To thee, my delight, in the evening I come:
No matter what beauties I saw in my way;
    They were but my visits, but thou art my home.

Then finish, dear Cloe, this pastoral war;
    And let us, like Horace and Lydia, agree:
For thou art a girl as much brighter than her,
    As he was a poet sublimer than me.

MATTHEW PRIOR

A Description of a City Shower

Careful observers may foretell the hour
(By sure prognostics) when to dread a show'r:
While rain depends, the pensive cat gives o'er
Her frolics, and pursues her tail no more.
Returning home at night, you'll find the sink
Strike your offended sense with double stink.
If you be wise, then go not far to dine,
You spend in coach-hire more than save in wine.
A coming show'r your shooting corns presage,
Old aches throb, your hollow tooth will rage.

6

Saunt'ring in coffee-house is Dulman seen;
He damns the climate, and complains of spleen.

  Meanwhile the South, rising with dabbled wings,
A sable cloud athwart the welkin flings,
That swilled more liquor than it could contain,
And like a drunkard gives it up again.
Brisk Susan whips her linen from the rope,
While the first drizzling show'r is borne aslope;
Such is that sprinkling which some careless quean
Flirts on you from her mop, but not so clean.
You fly, invoke the gods; then turning, stop
To rail; she singing, still whirls on her mop.
Not yet the dust had shunned th' unequal strife,
But aided by the wind, fought still for life;
And wafted with its foe by violent gust,
'Twas doubtful which was rain, and which was dust.
Ah! where must needy poet seek for aid,
When dust and rain at once his coat invade?
Sole coat, where dust cemented by the rain
Erects the nap, and leaves a cloudy stain.

  Now in contiguous drops the flood comes down,
Threat'ning with deluge this devoted town.
To shops in crowds the daggled females fly,
Pretend to cheapen goods, but nothing buy.
The Templar spruce, while ev'ry spout's a-broach,
Stays till 'tis fair, yet seems to call a coach.
The tucked-up sempstress walks with hasty strides,
While streams run down her oiled umbrella's sides.
Here various kinds, by various fortunes led,
Commence acquaintance underneath a shed.
Triumphant Tories and desponding Whigs
Forget their feuds, and join to save their wigs.
Boxed in a chair the beau impatient sits,
While spouts run clatt'ring o'er the roof by fits;
And ever and anon with frightful din
The leather sounds, he trembles from within.
So when Troy chair-men bore the wooden steed,
Pregnant with Greeks impatient to be freed

(Those bully Greeks, who, as the moderns do,
Instead of paying chair-men, run them through),
Laocoön struck the outside with his spear,
And each imprisoned hero quaked for fear.

   Now from all parts the swelling kennels flow,
And bear their trophies with them as they go:
Filth of all hues and odours seem to tell
What streets they sailed from, by the sight and smell.
They, as each torrent drives, with rapid force
From Smithfield or St Pulchre's shape their course,
And in huge confluent join at Snow Hill ridge,
Fall from the Conduit prone to Holborn Bridge.
Sweepings from butchers' stalls, dung, guts, and blood,
Drowned puppies, stinking sprats, all drenched in mud,
Dead cats and turnip-tops come tumbling down the flood.

JONATHAN SWIFT

from *The Rape of the Lock*

CANTO II

Not with more glories, in th' ethereal plain,
The sun first rises o'er the purpled main,
Than, issuing forth, the rival of his beams
Launched on the bosom of the silver Thames.
Fair nymphs and well-dressed youths around her shone,
But ev'ry eye was fixed on her alone.
On her white breast a sparkling cross she wore,
Which Jews might kiss, and infidels adore.
Her lively looks a sprightly mind disclose,
Quick as her eyes, and as unfixed as those:
Favours to none, to all she smiles extends;
Oft she rejects, but never once offends.
Bright as the sun, her eyes the gazers strike,
And, like the sun, they shine on all alike.

Yet graceful ease, and sweetness void of pride,
Might hide her faults, if belles had faults to hide:
If to her share some female errors fall,
Look on her face, and you'll forget 'em all.

This nymph, to the destruction of mankind,
Nourished two locks, which graceful hung behind
In equal curls, and well conspired to deck
With shining ringlets the smooth iv'ry neck.
Love in these labyrinths his slaves detains,
And mighty hearts are held in slender chains.
With hairy springes we the birds betray,
Slight lines of hair surprise the finny prey,
Fair tresses man's imperial race insnare,
And beauty draws us with a single hair.

Th' advent'rous baron the bright locks admired;
He saw, he wished, and to the prize aspired.
Resolved to win, he meditates the way,
By force to ravish, or by fraud betray;
For when success a lover's toil attends,
Few ask, if fraud or force attained his ends.

For this, ere Phoebus rose, he had implored
Propitious heav'n, and every pow'r adored,
But chiefly Love – to Love an altar built,
Of twelve vast French romances, neatly gilt.
There lay three garters, half a pair of gloves;
And all the trophies of his former loves.
With tender billet-doux he lights the pyre,
And breathes three am'rous sighs to raise the fire.
Then prostrate falls, and begs with ardent eyes
Soon to obtain, and long possess the prize:
The pow'rs gave ear, and granted half his pray'r,
The rest, the winds dispersed in empty air.

But now secure the painted vessel glides,
The sunbeams trembling on the floating tides,
While melting music steals upon the sky,
And softened sounds along the waters die.
Smooth flow the waves, the zephyrs gently play,
Belinda smiled, and all the world was gay.

All but the Sylph – with careful thoughts oppressed,
Th' impending woe sat heavy on his breast.
He summons straight his denizens of air;
The lucid squadrons round the sails repair:
Soft o'er the shrouds aerial whispers breathe,
That seemed but zephyrs to the train beneath.
Some to the sun their insect-wings unfold,
Waft on the breeze, or sink in clouds of gold.
Transparent forms, too fine for mortal sight,
Their fluid bodies half dissolved in light.
Loose to the wind their airy garments flew,
Thin glitt'ring textures of the filmy dew,
Dipped in the richest tincture of the skies,
Where light disports in ever-mingling dyes,
While ev'ry beam new transient colours flings,
Colours that change whene'er they wave their wings.
Amid the circle on the gilded mast,
Superior by the head, was Ariel placed;
His purple pinions opening to the sun,
He raised his azure wand, and thus begun:

   'Ye Sylphs and Sylphids, to your chief give ear;
Fays, fairies, genii, elves, and daemons hear!
Ye know the spheres and various tasks assigned
By laws eternal to th' aerial kind.
Some in the fields of purest ether play,
And bask and whiten in the blaze of day.
Some guide the course of wand'ring orbs on high,
Or roll the planets through the boundless sky.
Some less refined, beneath the moon's pale light
Pursue the stars that shoot athwart the night,
Or suck the mists in grosser air below,
Or dip their pinions in the painted bow,
Or brew fierce tempests on the wintry main,
Or o'er the glebe distil the kindly rain.
Others on earth o'er human race preside,
Watch all their ways, and all their actions guide:
Of these the chief the care of nations own,
And guard with arms divine the British throne.

'Our humbler province is to tend the fair,
Not a less pleasing, though less glorious care;
To save the powder from too rude a gale,
Nor let th' imprisoned essences exhale,
To draw fresh colours from the vernal flow'rs,
To steal from rainbows, ere they drop in showers,
A brighter wash; to curl their waving hairs,
Assist their blushes, and inspire their airs;
Nay oft, in dreams, invention we bestow,
To change a flounce, or add a furbelow.

'This day, black omens threat the brightest fair
That e'er deserved a watchful spirit's care;
Some dire disaster, or by force or slight,
But what, or where, the Fates have wrapped in night.
Whether the nymph shall break Diana's law,
Or some frail china jar receive a flaw,
Or stain her honour, or her new brocade,
Forget her pray'rs, or miss a masquerade,
Or lose her heart, or necklace, at a ball;
Or whether heav'n has doomed that Shock must fall.
Haste, then, ye spirits! to your charge repair;
The flutt'ring fan be Zephyretta's care;
The drops to thee, Brillante, we consign;
And, Momentilla, let the watch be thine;
Do thou, Crispissa, tend her fav'rite lock;
Ariel himself shall be the guard of Shock.

'To fifty chosen Sylphs, of special note,
We trust th' important charge, the petticoat:
Oft have we known that sev'n-fold fence to fail,
Though stiff with hoops, and armed with ribs of whale;
Form a strong line about the silver bound,
And guard the wide circumference around.

'Whatever spirit, careless of his charge,
His post neglects, or leaves the fair at large,
Shall feel sharp vengeance soon o'ertake his sins,
Be stopped in vials, or transfixed with pins;
Or plunged in lakes of bitter washes lie,
Or wedged whole ages in a bodkin's eye:

Gums and pomatums shall his flight restrain,
While clogged he beats his silken wings in vain;
Or alum-styptics with contracting power
Shrink his thin essence like a rivelled flower:
Or, as Ixion fixed, the wretch shall feel
The giddy motion of the whirling mill,
In fumes of burning chocolate shall glow,
And tremble at the sea that froths below!'

He spoke; the spirits from the sails descend;
Some, orb in orb, around the nymph extend,
Some thrid the mazy ringlets of her hair,
Some hang upon the pendants of her ear;
With beating hearts the dire event they wait,
Anxious and trembling for the birth of Fate.

ALEXANDER POPE

To Mr Gay, Who Wrote Him a Congratulatory Letter on the Finishing His House

Ah, friend! 'tis true – this truth you lovers know –
In vain my structures rise, my gardens grow;
In vain fair Thames reflects the double scenes
Of hanging mountains and of sloping greens:
Joy lives not here; to happier seats it flies,
And only dwells where Wortley casts her eyes.
What are the gay parterre, the chequered shade,
The morning bower, the ev'ning colonnade,
But soft recesses of uneasy minds,
To sigh unheard in to the passing winds?
So the struck deer in some sequestered part
Lies down to die, the arrow at his heart;
There, stretched unseen in coverts hid from day,
Bleeds drop by drop, and pants his life away.

ALEXANDER POPE

from *Epistle to Bathurst: Sir Balaam*

. . . Where London's column, pointing at the skies,
Like a tall bully, lifts the head, and lies;
There dwelt a Citizen of sober fame,
A plain good man, and Balaam was his name;
Religious, punctual, frugal, and so forth;
His word would pass for more than he was worth.
One solid dish his weekday meal affords,
An added pudding solemnized the Lord's:
Constant at Church, and Change; his gains were sure,
His givings rare, save farthings to the poor.

The Devil was piqued such saintship to behold,
And longed to tempt him like good Job of old:
But Satan now is wiser than of yore,
And tempts by making rich, not making poor.

Roused by the Prince of Air, the whirlwinds sweep
The surge, and plunge his Father in the deep;
Then full against his Cornish lands they roar,
And two rich shipwrecks bless the lucky shore.

Sir Balaam now, he lives like other folks,
He takes his chirping pint, and cracks his jokes:
'Live like yourself,' was soon my Lady's word;
And lo! two puddings smok'd upon the board.

Asleep and naked as an Indian lay,
An honest factor stole a Gem away:
He pledged it to the knight; the knight had wit,
So kept the Diamond, and the rogue was bit.
Some scruple rose, but thus he eased his thought,
'I'll now give sixpence where I gave a groat,
Where once I went to church, I'll now go twice –
And am so clear too of all other vice.'

The Tempter saw his time; the work he plied;
Stocks and Subscriptions pour on every side,
'Till all the Demon makes his full descent,
In one abundant shower of Cent per Cent,
Sinks deep within him, and possesses whole,
Then dubs Director, and secures his soul.

Behold Sir Balaam, now a man of spirit,
Ascribes his gettings to his parts and merit,
What late he called a Blessing, now was Wit,
And God's good Providence, a lucky Hit.
Things change their titles, as our manners turn;
His Compting-house employed the Sunday morn;
Seldom at Church ('twas such a busy life)
But duly sent his family and wife.
There (so the Devil ordained) one Christmas-tide
My good old Lady catched a cold, and died.

   A Nymph of Quality admires our Knight;
He marries, bows at Court, and grows polite:
Leaves the dull Cits, and joins (to please the fair)
The well-bred cuckolds in St James's air:
First, for his Son a gay Commission buys,
Who drinks, whores, fights, and in a duel dies:
His daughter flaunts a Viscount's tawdry wife;
She bears a Coronet and Pox for life.
In Britain's Senate he a seat obtains,
And one more Pensioner St Stephen gains.
My Lady falls to play; so bad her chance,
He must repair it; takes a bribe from France;
The House impeach him; Coningsby harangues;
The Court forsake him, and Sir Balaam hangs:
Wife, son, and daughter, Satan, are thy own,
His wealth, yet dearer, forfeit to the Crown:
The Devil and the King divide the prize,
And sad Sir Balaam curses God and dies.

ALEXANDER POPE

Ode on Solitude

   Happy the man, whose wish and care
      A few paternal acres bound,
   Content to breathe his native air,
      In his own ground.

Whose herds with milk, whose fields with bread,
    Whose flocks supply him with attire,
Whose trees in summer yield him shade,
        In winter fire.

Blest, who can unconcern'dly find
    Hours, days, and years slide soft away,
In health of body, peace of mind,
        Quiet by day,

Sound sleep by night; study and ease,
    Together mixt; sweet recreation;
And innocence, which most does please
        With meditation.

Thus let me live, unseen, unknown,
    Thus unlamented let me die,
Steal from the world, and not a stone
        Tell where I lie.

ALEXANDER POPE

A Nocturnal Reverie

In such a night, when every louder wind
Is to its distant cavern safe confined;
And only gentle Zephyr fans his wings,
And lonely Philomel, still waking, sings;
Or from some tree, famed for the owl's delight,
She, hollowing clear, directs the wand'rer right;
In such a night, when passing clouds give place,
Or thinly veil the heaven's mysterious face;
When in some river overhung with green,
The waving moon and trembling leaves are seen;
When freshened grass now bears itself upright,
And makes cool banks to pleasing rest invite,
Whence springs the woodbind and the bramble-rose,
And where the sleepy cowslip sheltered grows;

Whilst now a paler hue the foxglove takes,
Yet chequers still with red the dusky brakes;
When scattered glow-worms, but in twilight fine,
Show trivial beauties, watch their hour to shine;
Whilst Salisb'ry stands the test of every light,
In perfect charms and perfect virtue bright;
When odours, which declined repelling day,
Through temp'rate air uninterrupted stray;
When darkened groves their softest shadows wear,
And falling waters we distinctly hear;
When through the gloom more venerable shows
Some ancient fabric, awful in repose,
While sunburnt hills their swarthy looks conceal,
And swelling haycocks thicken up the vale;
When the loosed horse now, as his pasture leads,
Comes slowly grazing through th' adjoining meads,
Whose stealing pace and lengthened shade we fear,
Till torn-up forage in his teeth we hear;
When nibbling sheep at large pursue their food,
And unmolested kine rechew the cud;
When curlews cry beneath the village walls,
And to her straggling brood the partridge calls;
Their short-lived jubilee the creatures keep,
Which but endures whilst tyrant man does sleep;
When a sedate content the spirit feels,
And no fierce light disturbs, whilst it reveals,
But silent musings urge the mind to seek
Something too high for syllables to speak;
Till the free soul to a compos'dness charmed,
Finding the elements of rage disarmed,
O'er all below a solemn quiet grown,
Joys in th' inferior world and thinks it like her own:
In such a night let me abroad remain,
Till morning breaks, and all's confused again:
Our cares, our toils, our clamours are renewed,
Or pleasures, seldom reached, again pursued.

ANNE FINCH, COUNTESS OF WINCHILSEA

A Receipt to Cure the Vapours

Why will Delia thus retire,
    And idly languish life away?
While the sighing crowd admire,
    'Tis too soon for hartshorn tea.

All those dismal looks and fretting
    Cannot Damon's life restore;
Long ago the worms have ate him,
    You can never see him more.

Once again consult your toilette,
    In the glass your face review:
So much weeping soon will spoil it,
    And no spring your charms renew.

I, like you, was born a woman,
    Well I know what vapours mean:
The disease, alas! is common;
    Single, we have all the spleen.

All the morals that they tell us
    Never cured the sorrow yet:
Choose, among the pretty fellows,
    One of honour, youth and wit.

Prithee hear him every morning,
    At the least an hour or two;
Once again at night returning –
    I believe the dose will do.

LADY MARY WORTLEY MONTAGU

from *Epistle to a Lady: Of the Characters of Women*

Nothing so true as what you once let fall:
'Most women have no characters at all.'
Matter too soft a lasting mark to bear,
And best distinguished by black, brown, or fair.

　How many pictures of one nymph we view,
All how unlike each other, all how true!
Arcadia's Countess, here, in ermined pride,
Is there, Pastora by a fountain side.
Here Fannia, leering on her own good man,
And there, a naked Leda with a swan.
Let then the fair one beautifully cry
In Magdalen's loose hair and lifted eye,
Or dressed in smiles of sweet Cecilia shine,
With simp'ring angels, palms, and harps divine;
Whether the charmer sinner it, or saint it,
If folly grows romantic, I must paint it.

　Come then, the colours and the ground prepare!
Dip in the rainbow, trick her off in air,
Choose a firm cloud before it fall, and in it
Catch, ere she change, the Cynthia of this minute.

　Rufa, whose eye quick-glancing o'er the park
Attracts each light gay meteor of a spark,
Agrees as ill with Rufa studying Locke,
As Sappho's diamonds with her dirty smock,
Or Sappho at her toilet's greasy task,
With Sappho fragrant at an evening mask:
So morning insects, that in muck begun,
Shine, buzz, and fly-blow in the setting sun.

　How soft is Silia! fearful to offend,
The frail one's advocate, the weak one's friend:
To her, Calista proved her conduct nice,
And good Simplicius asks of her advice.
Sudden, she storms! she raves! You tip the wink,
But spare your censure – Silia does not drink.

All eyes may see from what the change arose,
All eyes may see – a pimple on her nose.

Papillia, wedded to her doting spark,
Sighs for the shades – 'How charming is a park!'
A park is purchased, but the fair he sees
All bathed in tears – 'Oh odious, odious trees!'

Ladies, like variegated tulips, show,
'Tis to their changes that their charms we owe;
Their happy spots the nice admirer take,
Fine by defect, and delicately weak.
'Twas thus Calypso once each heart alarmed,
Awed without virtue, without beauty charmed;
Her tongue bewitched as oddly as her eyes,
Less wit than mimic, more a wit than wise;
Strange graces still, and stranger flights she had,
Was just not ugly, and was just not mad;
Yet ne'er so sure our passion to create,
As when she touched the brink of all we hate.

Narcissa's nature, tolerably mild,
To make a wash would hardly stew a child,
Has ev'n been proved to grant a lover's pray'r,
And paid a tradesman once to make him stare;
Gave alms at Easter, in a Christian trim,
And made a widow happy for a whim.
Why then declare good-nature is her scorn,
When 'tis by that alone she can be borne?
Why pique all mortals, yet affect a name?
A fool to pleasure, and a slave to fame:
Now deep in Taylor and the Book of Martyrs,
Now drinking citron with his Grace and Chartres.
Now conscience chills her, and now passion burns;
And atheism and religion take their turns;
A very heathen in the carnal part,
Yet still a sad, good Christian at her heart.

See sin in state, majestically drunk,
Proud as a peeress, prouder as a punk;
Chaste to her husband, frank to all beside,
A teeming mistress, but a barren bride.

What then? let blood and body bear the fault,
Her head's untouched, that noble seat of thought:
Such this day's doctrine – in another fit
She sins with poets through pure love of wit.
What has not fired her bosom or her brain?
Caesar and Tall-boy, Charles and Charlemagne.
As Helluo, late dictator of the feast,
The nose of *haut-goût* and the tip of taste,
Critiqued your wine, and analysed your meat,
Yet on plain pudding deigned at home to eat;
So Philomedé, lect'ring all mankind
On the soft passion, and the taste refined,
Th' address, the delicacy – stoops at once,
And makes her hearty meal upon a dunce.

Flavia's a wit, has too much sense to pray;
To toast our wants and wishes is her way;
Nor asks of God, but of her stars, to give
The mighty blessing, 'while we live, to live.'
Then all for death, that opiate of the soul!
Lucretia's dagger, Rosamonda's bowl.
Say, what can cause such impotence of mind?
A spark too fickle, or a spouse too kind.
Wise wretch! with pleasures too refined to please,
With too much spirit to be e'er at ease,
With too much quickness ever to be taught,
With too much thinking to have common thought:
Who purchase pain with all that joy can give,
And die of nothing but a rage to live.

Turn then from wits; and look on Simo's mate,
No ass so meek, no ass so obstinate;
Or her that owns her faults, but never mends,
Because she's honest, and the best of friends;
Or her whose life the church and scandal share,
For ever in a passion, or a pray'r;
Or her who laughs at hell, but (like her Grace)
Cries, 'Ah! how charming if there's no such place!';
Or who in sweet vicissitude appears
Of mirth and opium, ratafie and tears,

The daily anodyne, and nightly draught,
To kill those foes to fair ones, time and thought.
Woman and fool are two hard things to hit,
For true no-meaning puzzles more than wit.

   But what are these to great Atossa's mind?
Scarce once herself, by turns all womankind!
Who, with herself, or others, from her birth
Finds all her life one warfare upon earth:
Shines in exposing knaves and painting fools,
Yet is whate'er she hates and ridicules.
No thought advances, but her eddy brain
Whisks it about, and down it goes again.
Full sixty years the world has been her trade,
The wisest fool much time has ever made.
From loveless youth to unrespected age,
No passion gratified except her rage,
So much the fury still outran the wit,
The pleasure missed her, and the scandal hit.
Who breaks with her, provokes revenge from hell,
But he's a bolder man who dares be well:
Her ev'ry turn with violence pursued,
Nor more a storm her hate than gratitude.
To that each passion turns, or soon or late;
Love, if it makes her yield, must make her hate:
Superiors? death! and equals? what a curse!
But an inferior not dependant? worse.
Offend her, and she knows not to forgive;
Oblige her, and she'll hate you while you live:
But die, and she'll adore you – then the bust
And temple rise – then fall again to dust.
Last night, her lord was all that's good and great,
A knave this morning, and his will a cheat.
Strange! by the means defeated of the ends,
By spirit robbed of pow'r, by warmth of friends,
By wealth of follow'rs! without one distress,
Sick of herself through very selfishness!
Atossa, cursed with ev'ry granted pray'r,
Childless with all her children, wants an heir.

To heirs unknown descends th' unguarded store,
Or wanders, heav'n-directed, to the poor.

Pictures like these, dear Madam, to design,
Asks no firm hand, and no unerring line;
Some wand'ring touch, or some reflected light,
Some flying stroke alone can hit 'em right:
For how should equal colours do the knack?
Chameleons who can paint in white and black?

'Yet Cloe sure was formed without a spot.' –
Nature in her then erred not, but forgot.
'With every pleasing, every prudent part,
Say, what can Cloe want?' – She wants a heart.
She speaks, behaves, and acts, just as she ought,
But never, never reached one gen'rous thought.
Virtue she finds too painful an endeavour,
Content to dwell in decencies for ever.
So very reasonable, so unmoved,
As never yet to love, or to be loved.
She, while her lover pants upon her breast,
Can mark the figures on an Indian chest;
And when she sees her friend in deep despair,
Observes how much a chintz exceeds mohair.
Forbid it, heav'n, a favour or a debt
She e'er should cancel – but she may forget.
Safe is your secret still in Cloe's ear;
But none of Cloe's shall you ever hear.
Of all her dears she never slandered one,
But cares not if a thousand are undone.
Would Cloe know if you're alive or dead?
She bids her footman put it in her head.
Cloe is prudent – would you too be wise?
Then never break your heart when Cloe dies.

ALEXANDER POPE

A Short Song of Congratulation

Long-expected one and twenty
  Ling'ring year at last is flown;
Pomp and pleasure, pride and plenty,
  Great Sir John, are all your own.

Loosened from the minor's tether,
  Free to mortgage or to sell,
Wild as wind and light as feather,
  Bid the slaves of thrift farewell.

Call the Bettys, Kates and Jennys,
  Ev'ry name that laughs at care;
Lavish of your grandsire's guineas,
  Show the spirit of an heir.

All that prey on vice and folly
  Joy to see their quarry fly:
Here the gamester light and jolly,
  There the lender grave and sly.

Wealth, Sir John, was made to wander,
  Let it wander as it will;
See the jockey, see the pander,
  Bid them come, and take their fill.

When the bonny blade carouses,
  Pockets full, and spirits high,
What are acres? What are houses?
  Only dirt, or wet or dry.

If the guardian or the mother
  Tell the woes of wilful waste,
Scorn their counsel and their pother,
  You can hang or drown at last.

SAMUEL JOHNSON

23

A Satirical Elegy on the Death of a Late Famous General

His Grace! impossible! what, dead!
Of old age too, and in his bed!
And could that Mighty Warrior fall?
And so inglorious, after all!
Well, since he's gone, no matter how,
The last loud trump must wake him now:
And, trust me, as the noise grows stronger,
He'd wish to sleep a little longer.
And could he be indeed so old
As by the newspapers we're told?
Threescore, I think, is pretty high;
'Twas time in conscience he should die.
This world he cumbered long enough;
He burnt his candle to the snuff;
And that's the reason, some folks think,
He left behind *so great a stink*.
Behold his funeral appears,
Nor widow's sighs, nor orphan's tears,
Wont at such times each heart to pierce,
Attend the progress of his hearse.
But what of that, his friends may say,
He had those honours in his day.
True to his profit and his pride,
He made them weep before he died.

  Come hither, all ye empty things,
Ye bubbles raised by breath of kings;
Who float upon the tide of state,
Come hither, and behold your fate.
Let pride be taught by this rebuke,
How very mean a thing's a Duke;
From all his ill-got honours flung,
Turned to that dirt from whence he sprung.

JONATHAN SWIFT

from *An Epistle to Richard Boyle, Earl of Burlington*

At Timon's villa let us pass a day,
Where all cry out, 'What sums are thrown away!'
So proud, so grand, of that stupendous air,
Soft and agreeable come never there.
Greatness, with Timon, dwells in such a draught
As brings all Brobdignag before your thought.
To compass this, his building is a town,
His pond an ocean, his parterre a down:
Who but must laugh, the master when he sees,
A puny insect, shiv'ring at a breeze!
Lo, what huge heaps of littleness around!
The whole, a laboured quarry above ground.
Two Cupids squirt before: a lake behind
Improves the keenness of the northern wind.
His gardens next your admiration call,
On ev'ry side you look, behold the wall!
No pleasing intricacies intervene,
No artful wildness to perplex the scene;
Grove nods at grove, each alley has a brother,
And half the platform just reflects the other.
The suff'ring eye inverted nature sees,
Trees cut to statues, statues thick as trees,
With here a fountain, never to be played,
And there a summer-house, that knows no shade;
Here Amphitrite sails through myrtle bow'rs;
There gladiators fight, or die, in flow'rs;
Unwatered see the drooping sea-horse mourn,
And swallows roost in Nilus' dusty urn.
    My Lord advances with majestic mien,
Smit with the mighty pleasure to be seen:
But soft – by regular approach – not yet –
First through the length of yon hot terrace sweat,
And when up ten steep slopes you've dragged your thighs,
Just at his study-door he'll bless your eyes.
    His study! with what authors is it stored?

In books, not authors, curious is my Lord;
To all their dated backs he turns you round;
These Aldus printed, those Du Sueïl has bound.
Lo, some are vellum, and the rest as good
For all his Lordship knows, but they are wood.
For Locke or Milton 'tis in vain to look,
These shelves admit not any modern book.

And now the chapel's silver bell you hear,
That summons you to all the pride of pray'r:
Light quirks of music, broken and uneven,
Make the soul dance upon a jig to heaven.
On painted ceilings you devoutly stare,
Where sprawl the saints of Verrio or Laguerre,
On gilded clouds in fair expansion lie,
And bring all paradise before your eye.
To rest, the cushion and soft dean invite,
Who never mentions hell to ears polite.

But hark! the chiming clocks to dinner call;
A hundred footsteps scrape the marble hall:
The rich buffet well-coloured serpents grace,
And gaping Tritons spew to wash your face.
Is this a dinner? this a genial room?
No, 'tis a temple, and a hecatomb.
A solemn sacrifice, performed in state,
You drink by measure, and to minutes eat.
So quick retires each flying course, you'd swear
Sancho's dread doctor and his wand were there.
Between each act the trembling salvers ring,
From soup to sweet-wine, and God bless the King.
In plenty starving, tantalised in state,
And complaisantly helped to all I hate,
Treated, caressed, and tired, I take my leave,
Sick of his civil pride from morn to eve;
I curse such lavish cost, and little skill,
And swear no day was ever passed so ill.

Yet hence the poor are clothed, the hungry fed;
Health to himself, and to his infants bread,
The lab'rer bears: what his hard heart denies,

His charitable vanity supplies.
    Another age shall see the golden ear
Imbrown the slope, and nod on the parterre,
Deep harvests bury all his pride has planned,
And laughing Ceres reassume the land.

ALEXANDER POPE

The Dying Christian to His Soul

Vital spark of heav'nly flame!
Quit, oh quit this mortal frame:
Trembling, hoping, ling'ring, flying,
Oh the pain, the bliss of dying!
Cease, fond Nature, cease thy strife,
And let me languish into life.

Hark! they whisper; Angels say,
'Sister Spirit, come away!'
What is this absorbs me quite?
Steals my senses, shuts my sight,
Drowns my spirits, draws my breath?
Tell me, my Soul, can this be Death?

The world recedes; it disappears!
Heav'n opens on my eyes! my ears
With sounds seraphic ring:
Lend, lend your wings! I mount! I fly!
O Grave! where is thy Victory?
O Death! where is thy Sting?

ALEXANDER POPE

The Day of Judgement. An Ode

Attempted in English Sapphic

When the fierce north wind with his airy forces
Rears up the Baltic to a foaming fury,
And the red lightning with a storm of hail comes
        Rushing amain down,

How the poor sailors stand amazed and tremble!
While the hoarse thunder like a bloody trumpet
Roars a loud onset to the gaping waters
        Quick to devour them.

Such shall the noise be, and the wild disorder,
(If things eternal may be like these earthly)
Such the dire terror when the great archangel
        Shakes the creation;

Tears the strong pillars of the vault of heaven,
Breaks up old marble, the repose of princes;
See the graves open, and the bones arising,
        Flames all around 'em.

Hark the shrill outcries of the guilty wretches!
Lively bright horror and amazing anguish
Stare through their eye-lids, while the living worm lies
        Gnawing within them.

Thoughts like old vultures prey upon their heartstrings,
And the smart twinges, when their eye beholds the
Lofty Judge frowning, and the flood of vengeance
        Rolling afore him.

Hopeless immortals! how they scream and shiver
While devils push them to the pit wide yawning
Hideous and gloomy, to receive them headlong
        Down to the centre.

Stop here, my fancy (all away, ye horrid
Doleful ideas): come arise to Jesus,

How he sits god-like! and the saints around him
        Throned, yet adoring!

O may I sit there when he comes triumphant
Dooming the nations: then ascend to glory,
While our hosannahs all along the passage
        Shout the Redeemer.

                                        ISAAC WATTS

On the Death of Dr Robert Levet

Condemned to hope's delusive mine,
    As on we toil from day to day,
By sudden blasts, or slow decline,
    Our social comforts drop away.

Well tried through many a varying year,
    See Levet to the grave descend;
Officious, innocent, sincere,
    Of ev'ry friendless name the friend.

Yet still he fills affection's eye,
    Obscurely wise, and coarsely kind;
Nor, lettered arrogance, deny
    Thy praise to merit unrefined.

When fainting nature called for aid,
    And hov'ring death prepared the blow,
His vig'rous remedy displayed
    The power of art without the show.

In misery's darkest caverns known,
    His useful care was ever nigh,
Where hopeless anguish poured his groan,
    And lonely want retired to die.

No summons mocked by chill delay,
    No petty gain disdained by pride,
The modest wants of ev'ry day
    The toil of ev'ry day supplied.

His virtues walked their narrow round,
  Nor made a pause, nor left a void;
And sure th' Eternal Master found
  The single talent well employed.

The busy day, the peaceful night,
  Unfelt, uncounted, glided by;
His frame was firm, his powers were bright,
  Though now his eightieth year was nigh.

Then with no throbbing fiery pain,
  No cold gradations of decay,
Death broke at once the vital chain,
  And freed his soul the nearest way.

SAMUEL JOHNSON

from *The Death of Dr Swift*

  The time is not remote, when I
Must by the course of nature die;
When I foresee my special friends
Will try to find their private ends,
Though it is hardly understood
Which way my death can do them good;
Yet thus, methinks, I hear 'em speak:
'See, how the Dean begins to break:
Poor gentleman, he droops apace,
You plainly find it in his face;
That old vertigo in his head
Will never leave him, till he's dead.
Besides, his memory decays,
He recollects not what he says;
He cannot call his friends to mind,
Forgets the place where last he dined;
Plies you with stories o'er and o'er:
He told them fifty times before.

How does he fancy we can sit
To hear his out-of-fashioned wit?
But he takes up with younger folks,
Who for his wine will bear his jokes:
Faith, he must make his stories shorter,
Or change his comrades once a quarter;
In half the time, he talks them round;
There must another set be found.

   'For poetry, he's past his prime,
He takes an hour to find a rhyme:
His fire is out, his wit decayed,
His fancy sunk, his Muse a jade.
I'd have him throw away his pen;
But there's no talking to some men.'

   And then their tenderness appears,
By adding largely to my years:
'He's older than he would be reckoned,
And well remembers Charles the Second.

   'He hardly drinks a pint of wine;
And that, I doubt, is no good sign.
His stomach too begins to fail:
Last year we thought him strong and hale;
But now he's quite another thing;
I wish he may hold out till spring.'

   Then hug themselves, and reason thus:
'It is not yet so bad with us.'

   In such a case they talk in tropes,
And by their fears express their hopes;
Some great misfortune to portend,
No enemy can match a friend.
With all the kindness they profess,
The merit of a lucky guess
(When daily howd'y's come of course,
And servants answer, 'Worse and worse')
Would please 'em better than to tell
That, God be praised, the Dean is well.
Then he who prophesied the best
Approves his foresight to the rest:

'You know, I always feared the worst,
And often told you so at first.'
He'd rather choose that I should die
Than his prediction prove a lie.
Not one foretells I shall recover;
But all agree to give me over.

Suppose me dead; and then suppose
A club assembled at the Rose,
Where, from discourse of this and that,
I grow the subject of their chat;
And, while they toss my name about,
With favour some, and some without,
One quite indiff'rent in the cause
My character impartial draws:
'The Dean, if we believe report,
Was never ill received at court.
As for his works in verse and prose,
I own myself no judge of those;
Nor, can I tell what critics thought 'em,
But, this I know, all people bought 'em;
As with a moral view designed
To cure the vices of mankind,
His vein, ironically grave,
Exposed the fool, and lashed the knave;
To steal a hint was never known,
But what he writ was all his own.
'He never thought an honour done him,
Because a duke was proud to own him;
Would rather slip aside, and choose
To talk with wits in dirty shoes;
Despised the fools with Stars and Garters
So often seen caressing Chartres.
He never courted men in station,
Nor persons had in admiration;
Of no man's greatness was afraid,
Because he sought for no man's aid.
Though trusted long in great affairs,

He gave himself no haughty airs;
Without regarding private ends,
Spent all his credit for his friends,
And only chose the wise and good –
No flatterers; no allies in blood –
But succoured virtue in distress,
And seldom failed of good success;
As numbers in their hearts must own,
Who, but for him, had been unknown.

'With princes kept a due decorum,
But never stood in awe before 'em:
And to her Majesty, God bless her,
Would speak as free as to her dresser;
She thought it his peculiar whim,
Nor took it ill as come from him.
He followed David's lesson just,
In princes never put thy trust.
And, would you make him truly sour,
Provoke him with a slave in power.
The Irish Senate if you named,
With what impatience he declaimed!
Fair Liberty was all his cry;
For her he stood prepared to die;
For her he boldly stood alone;
For her he oft exposed his own.
Two kingdoms, just as faction led,
Had set a price upon his head;
But not a traitor could be found,
To sell him for six hundred pound.

'Had he but spared his tongue and pen,
He might have rose like other men:
But power was never in his thought;
And wealth he valued not a groat.
Ingratitude he often found,
And pitied those who meant the wound:
But kept the tenor of his mind,
To merit well of human kind,
Nor made a sacrifice of those

Who still were true, to please his foes.
He laboured many a fruitless hour
To reconcile his friends in power;
Saw mischief by a faction brewing,
While they pursued each other's ruin;
But, finding vain was all his care,
He left the court in mere despair.

'And, oh, how short are human schemes!
Here ended all our golden dreams.
What St John's skill in state affairs,
What Ormonde's valour, Oxford's cares,
To save their sinking country lent,
Was all destroyed by one event.
Too soon that precious life was ended,
On which alone our weal depended.
When up a dangerous faction starts,
With wrath and vengeance in their hearts;
By solemn league and covenant bound
To ruin, slaughter, and confound;
To turn religion to a fable,
And make the government a Babel;
Pervert the law, disgrace the gown,
Corrupt the senate, rob the crown;
To sacrifice old England's glory,
And make her infamous in story.
When such a tempest shook the land,
How could unguarded virtue stand?

'With horror, grief, despair the Dean
Beheld the dire destructive scene:
His friends in exile, or the Tower,
Himself within the frown of power;
Pursued by base envenomed pens
Far to the land of slaves and fens;
A servile race in folly nursed,
Who truckle most when treated worst.

'By innocence and resolution,
He bore continual persecution,
While numbers to preferment rose,

Whose merits were, to be his foes;
When ev'n his own familiar friends,
Intent upon their private ends,
Like renegadoes now he feels
Against him lifting up their heels.

'The Dean did by his pen defeat
An infamous destructive cheat;
Taught fools their int'rest how to know,
And gave them arms to ward the blow.
Envy hath owned it was his doing
To save that helpless land from ruin,
While they who at the steerage stood,
And reaped the profit, sought his blood.

'To save them from their evil fate,
In him was held a crime of state.
A wicked monster on the bench,
Whose fury blood could never quench,
As vile and profligate a villain
As modern Scroggs, or old Tresilian,
Who long all justice had discarded,
Nor feared he God, nor man regarded;
Vowed on the Dean his rage to vent,
And make him of his zeal repent;
But heav'n his innocence defends;
The grateful people stand his friends.
Not strains of law, nor judge's frown,
Nor topics brought to please the crown,
Nor witness hired, nor jury picked,
Prevail to bring him in convict.

'In exile with a steady heart,
He spent his life's declining part,
Where folly, pride, and faction sway,
Remote from St John, Pope, and Gay.

'His friendship there to few confined,
Were always of the middling kind:
No fools of rank, a mongrel breed,
Who fain would pass for lords indeed,
Where titles give no right or power,

And peerage is a withered flower;
He would have held it a disgrace,
If such a wretch had known his face.
On rural squires, that kingdom's bane,
He vented oft his wrath in vain:
Biennial squires, to market brought,
Who sell their souls and votes for naught;
The nation stripped, go joyful back,
To rob the church, their tenants rack,
Go snacks with thieves and rapparees,
And keep the peace, to pick up fees;
In every job to have a share,
A jail or barrack to repair;
And turn the tax for public roads
Commodious to their own abodes.

  'Perhaps I may allow the Dean
Had too much satire in his vein;
And seemed determined not to starve it,
Because no age could more deserve it.
Yet malice never was his aim;
He lashed the vice, but spared the name.
No individual could resent,
Where thousands equally were meant.
His satire points at no defect
But what all mortals may correct;
For he abhorred that senseless tribe
Who call it humour when they jibe.
He spared a hump or crooked nose
Whose owners set not up for beaux.
True genuine dullness moved his pity,
Unless it offered to be witty.
Those who their ignorance confessed
He ne'er offended with a jest;
But laughed to hear an idiot quote
A verse from Horace learned by rote.

  'He knew an hundred pleasant stories,
With all the turns of Whigs and Tories;
Was cheerful to his dying day,

And friends would let him have his way.
    'He gave the little wealth he had
To build a house for fools and mad,
And showed by one satiric touch,
No nation wanted it so much.
That kingdom he hath left his debtor;
I wish it soon may have a better.'

JONATHAN SWIFT

Ode

The spacious firmament on high,
With all the blue ethereal sky,
And spangled heav'ns, a shining frame,
Their great original proclaim:
Th' unwearied sun, from day to day,
Does his Creator's power display,
And publishes to every land
The work of an almighty hand.

Soon as the evening shades prevail,
The moon takes up the wondrous tale,
And nightly to the list'ning earth
Repeats the story of her birth:
Whilst all the stars that round her burn,
And all the planets in their turn,
Confirm the tidings as they roll,
And spread the truth from pole to pole.

What though, in solemn silence, all
Move round the dark terrestrial ball?
What though nor real voice nor sound
Amid their radiant orbs be found?
In reason's ear they all rejoice,
And utter forth a glorious voice,
For ever singing, as they shine,
'The hand that made us is divine.'

JOSEPH ADDISON

When I survey the wond'rous cross
On which the Prince of Glory died,
My richest gain I count but loss,
And pour contempt on all my pride.

Forbid it, Lord, that I should boast
Save in the death of Christ my God;
All the vain things that charm me most,
I sacrifice them to his blood.

See from his head, his hands, his feet,
Sorrow and love flow mingled down;
Did e'er such love and sorrow meet?
Or thorns compose so rich a crown?

His dying crimson like a robe
Spreads o'er his body on the tree;
Then am I dead to all the globe,
And all the globe is dead to me.

Were the whole realm of nature mine,
That were a present far too small;
Love so amazing, so divine,
Demands my soul, my life, my all.

ISAAC WATTS

Ode to Evening

If aught of oaten stop, or pastoral song,
May hope, chaste Eve, to soothe thy modest ear,
    Like thy own solemn springs,
    Thy springs and dying gales,
O nymph reserved, while now the bright-haired sun
Sits in yon western tent, whose cloudy skirts,
    With brede ethereal wove,

O'erhang his wavy bed;
Now air is hushed, save where the weak-eyed bat
With short shrill shriek flits by on leathern wing,
    Or where the beetle winds
    His small but sullen horn,
As oft he rises midst the twilight path,
Against the pilgrim borne in heedless hum:
    Now teach me, maid composed,
    To breathe some softened strain,
Whose numbers, stealing through thy dark'ning vale,
May not unseemly with its stillness suit,
    As, musing slow, I hail
    Thy genial loved return!
For when thy folding-star arising shows
His paly circlet, at his warning lamp
    The fragrant hours, and elves
    Who slept in flowers the day,
And many a nymph who wreathes her brows with sedge,
And sheds the fresh'ning dew, and, lovelier still,
    The pensive Pleasures sweet,
    Prepare thy shadowy car.
Then lead, calm vot'ress, where some sheety lake
Cheers the lone heath, or some time-hallowed pile,
    Or upland fallows grey,
    Reflect its last cool gleam.
But when chill blust'ring winds, or driving rain,
Forbid my willing feet, be mine the hut,
    That from the mountain's side
    Views wilds, and swelling floods,
And hamlets brown, and dim-discovered spires,
And hears their simple bell, and marks o'er all
    Thy dewy fingers draw
    The gradual dusky veil.
While Spring shall pour his show'rs, as oft he wont,
And bathe thy breathing tresses, meekest Eve!
    While Summer loves to sport
    Beneath thy ling'ring light;
While sallow Autumn fills thy lap with leaves,

Or Winter, yelling through the troublous air,
    Affrights thy shrinking train,
    And rudely rends thy robes;
So long, sure-found beneath the sylvan shed,
Shall Fancy, Friendship, Science, rose-lipped Health
    Thy gentlest influence own,
    And love thy fav'rite name!

WILLIAM COLLINS

Elegy Written in a Country Churchyard

The curfew tolls the knell of parting day,
The lowing herd wind slowly o'er the lea,
The ploughman homeward plods his weary way,
And leaves the world to darkness and to me.

Now fades the glimmering landscape on the sight,
And all the air a solemn stillness holds,
Save where the beetle wheels his droning flight,
And drowsy tinklings lull the distant folds;

Save that from yonder ivy-mantled tow'r
The moping owl does to the moon complain
Of such as, wand'ring near her secret bow'r,
Molest her ancient solitary reign.

Beneath those rugged elms, that yew-tree's shade,
Where heaves the turf in many a mould'ring heap,
Each in his narrow cell for ever laid,
The rude forefathers of the hamlet sleep.

The breezy call of incense-breathing morn,
The swallow twitt'ring from the straw-built shed,
The cock's shrill clarion or the echoing horn,
No more shall rouse them from their lowly bed.

For them no more the blazing hearth shall burn,
Or busy housewife ply her evening care:

No children run to lisp their sire's return,
Or climb his knees the envied kiss to share.

Oft did the harvest to their sickle yield,
Their furrow oft the stubborn glebe has broke;
How jocund did they drive their team afield!
How bowed the woods beneath their sturdy stroke!

Let not Ambition mock their useful toil,
Their homely joys and destiny obscure;
Nor Grandeur hear, with a disdainful smile,
The short and simple annals of the poor.

The boast of heraldry, the pomp of pow'r,
And all that beauty, all that wealth e'er gave,
Awaits alike the inevitable hour.
The paths of glory lead but to the grave.

Nor you, ye Proud, impute to these the fault,
If Mem'ry o'er their tomb no trophies raise,
Where through the long-drawn aisle and fretted vault
The pealing anthem swells the note of praise.

Can storied urn or animated bust
Back to its mansion call the fleeting breath?
Can Honour's voice provoke the silent dust,
Or Flatt'ry soothe the dull cold ear of Death?

Perhaps in this neglected spot is laid
Some heart once pregnant with celestial fire;
Hands that the rod of empire might have swayed,
Or waked to ecstasy the living lyre.

But Knowledge to their eyes her ample page
Rich with the spoils of time did ne'er unroll;
Chill Penury repressed their noble rage,
And froze the genial current of the soul.

Full many a gem of purest ray serene
The dark unfathomed caves of ocean bear:
Full many a flower is born to blush unseen
And waste its sweetness on the desert air.

Some village-Hampden that with dauntless breast
The little tyrant of his fields withstood;
Some mute inglorious Milton here may rest,
Some Cromwell guiltless of his country's blood.

Th' applause of list'ning senates to command,
The threats of pain and ruin to despise,
To scatter plenty o'er a smiling land,
And read their hist'ry in a nation's eyes,

Their lot forbade: nor circumscribed alone
Their growing virtues, but their crimes confined;
Forbade to wade through slaughter to a throne,
And shut the gates of mercy on mankind,

The struggling pangs of conscious truth to hide,
To quench the blushes of ingenuous shame,
Or heap the shrine of Luxury and Pride
With incense kindled at the Muse's flame.

Far from the madding crowd's ignoble strife
Their sober wishes never learned to stray;
Along the cool sequestered vale of life
They kept the noiseless tenor of their way.

Yet ev'n these bones from insult to protect
Some frail memorial still erected nigh,
With uncouth rhymes and shapeless sculpture decked,
Implores the passing tribute of a sigh.

Their name, their years, spelt by th' unlettered muse,
The place of fame and elegy supply:
And many a holy text around she strews,
That teach the rustic moralist to die.

For who to dumb Forgetfulness a prey,
This pleasing anxious being e'er resigned,
Left the warm precincts of the cheerful day,
Nor cast one longing ling'ring look behind?

On some fond breast the parting soul relies,
Some pious drops the closing eye requires;

Ev'n from the tomb the voice of Nature cries,
Ev'n in our ashes live their wonted fires.

For thee who, mindful of th' unhonoured dead,
Dost in these lines their artless tale relate;
If chance, by lonely Contemplation led,
Some kindred spirit shall inquire thy fate,

Haply some hoary-headed swain may say,
'Oft have we seen him at the peep of dawn
Brushing with hasty steps the dews away
To meet the sun upon the upland lawn.

'There at the foot of yonder nodding beech
That wreathes its old fantastic roots so high,
His listless length at noontide would he stretch,
And pore upon the brook that babbles by.

'Hard by yon wood, now smiling as in scorn,
Muttering his wayward fancies he would rove,
Now drooping, woeful wan, like one forlorn,
Or crazed with care, or crossed in hopeless love.

'One morn I missed him on the customed hill,
Along the heath and near his fav'rite tree;
Another came; nor yet beside the rill,
Nor up the lawn, nor at the wood was he;

'The next with dirges due in sad array
Slow through the church-way path we saw him borne.
Approach and read (for thou canst read) the lay,
Graved on the stone beneath yon aged thorn.'

THE EPITAPH

Here rests his head upon the lap of earth
A youth to fortune and to fame unknown:
Fair Science frown'd not on his humble birth
And Melancholy mark'd him for her own.

Large was his bounty, and his soul sincere,
Heav'n did a recompense as largely send:
He gave to Mis'ry all he had, a tear:
He gain'd from Heav'n ('twas all he wish'd) a friend.

No farther seek his merits to disclose,
Or draw his frailties from their dread abode
(There they alike in trembling hope repose)
The bosom of his Father and his God.

THOMAS GRAY

On a Favourite Cat, Drowned in a Tub of Gold Fishes

'Twas on a lofty vase's side,
Where China's gayest art had dyed
The azure flowers that blow,
Demurest of the tabby kind
The pensive Selima, reclined,
Gazed on the lake below.

Her conscious tail her joy declared:
The fair round face, the snowy beard,
The velvet of her paws,
Her coat that with the tortoise vies,
Her ears of jet, and emerald eyes –
She saw, and purr'd applause.

Still had she gazed, but 'midst the tide
Two angel forms were seen to glide,
The Genii of the stream:
Their scaly armour's Tyrian hue
Through richest purple, to the view
Betray'd a golden gleam.

The hapless Nymph with wonder saw:
A whisker first, and then a claw
With many an ardent wish
She stretch'd, in vain, to reach the prize –
What female heart can gold despise?
What Cat's averse to fish?

44

Presumptuous maid! with looks intent
Again she stretch'd, again she bent,
Nor knew the gulf between –
Malignant Fate sat by and smiled –
The slippery verge her feet beguiled;
She tumbled headlong in!

Eight times emerging from the flood
She mew'd to every watery God
Some speedy aid to send: –
No Dolphin came, no Nereid stirr'd,
Nor cruel Tom nor Susan heard –
A favourite has no friend!

From hence, ye Beauties! undeceived
Know one false step is ne'er retrieved,
And be with caution bold:
Not all that tempts your wandering eyes
And heedless hearts, is lawful prize,
Nor all that glisters, gold!

THOMAS GRAY

On L[or]d H[olland']s Seat near M[argat]e, K[en]t

Old and abandoned by each venal friend,
    Here H[olland] took the pious resolution
To smuggle some few years and strive to mend
    A broken character and constitution.
On this congenial spot he fixed his choice;
    Earl Godwin trembled for his neighbouring sand;
Here seagulls scream and cormorants rejoice,
    And mariners, though shipwrecked, dread to land.
Here reign the blust'ring North and blighting East,
    No tree is heard to whisper, bird to sing:
Yet nature cannot furnish out the feast,
    Art he invokes new horrors still to bring.

Now mould'ring fanes and battlements arise,
　　Arches and turrets nodding to their fall,
Unpeopled palaces delude his eyes,
　　And mimic desolation covers all.
'Ah', said the sighing peer, 'had Bute been true
　　Nor Shelburne's, Rigby's, Calcraft's friendship vain,
Far other scenes than these had blessed our view
　　And realized the ruins that we feign.
Purged by the sword and beautified by fire,
　　Then had we seen proud London's hated walls:
Owls might have hooted in St Peter's choir,
　　And foxes stunk and littered in St Paul's.'

THOMAS GRAY

A Translation of Benserade's Verse à son Lit

In bed we laugh, in bed we cry,
And born in bed, in bed we die;
The near approach a bed may shew
Of human bliss to human woe.

from *Jubilate Agno*

For I will consider my Cat Jeoffry.

For he is the servant of the Living God duly and daily serving him.

For at the first glance of the glory of God in the East he worships in his way.

For is this done by wreathing his body seven times round with elegant quickness.

For then he leaps up to catch the musk, which is the blessing of God upon his prayer.

For he rolls upon prank to work it in.

For having done duty and received blessing he begins to consider himself.

46

For this he performs in ten degrees.

For first he looks upon his fore-paws to see if they are clean.

For secondly he kicks up behind to clear away there.

For thirdly he works it upon stretch with the fore-paws extended.

For fourthly he sharpens his paws by wood.

For fifthly he washes himself.

For sixthly he rolls upon wash.

For seventhly he fleas himself, that he may not be interrupted upon the beat.

For eighthly he rubs himself against a post.

For ninthly he looks up for his instructions.

For tenthly he goes in quest of food.

For having consider'd God and himself he will consider his neighbour.

For if he meets another cat he will kiss her in kindness.

For when he takes his prey he plays with it to give it chance.

For one mouse in seven escapes by his dallying.

For when his day's work is done his business more properly begins.

For he keeps the Lord's watch in the night against the adversary.

For he counteracts the powers of darkness by his electrical skin and glaring eyes.

For he counteracts the Devil, who is death, by brisking about the life.

For in his morning orisons he loves the sun and the sun loves him.

For he is of the tribe of Tiger.

For the Cherub Cat is a term of the Angel Tiger.

For he has the subtlety and hissing of a serpent, which in goodness he suppresses.

For he will not do destruction, if he is well-fed, neither will he spit without provocation.

For he purrs in thankfulness, when God tells him he's a good Cat.

For he is an instrument for the children to learn benevolence upon.

For every house is incompleat without him and a blessing is lacking in the spirit.

For the Lord commanded Moses concerning the cats at the departure of the Children of Israel from Egypt.

For every family had one cat at least in the bag.

For the English Cats are the best in Europe.

For he is the cleanest in the use of his fore-paws of any quadrupede.

For the dexterity of his defence is an instance of the love of God to him exceedingly.

For he is the quickest to his mark of any creature.

For he is tenacious of his point.

For he is a mixture of gravity and waggery.

For he knows that God is his Saviour.

For there is nothing sweeter than his peace when at rest.

For there is nothing brisker than his life when in motion.

For he is of the Lord's poor and so indeed is he called by benevolence perpetually – Poor Jeoffry! poor Jeoffry! the rat has bit thy throat.

For I bless the name of the Lord Jesus that Jeoffry is better.

For the divine spirit comes about his body to sustain it in compleat cat.

For his tongue is exceeding pure so that it has in purity what it wants in musick.

For he is docile and can learn certain things.

For he can set up with gravity which is patience upon approbation.

For he can fetch and carry, which is patience in employment.

For he can jump over a stick which is patience upon proof positive.

For he can spraggle upon waggle at the word of command.

For he can jump from an eminence into his master's bosom.

For he can catch the cork and toss it again.

For he is hated by the hypocrite and miser.

For the former is affraid of detection.

For the latter refuses the charge.

For he camels his back to bear the first notion of business.

For he is good to think on, if a man would express himself neatly.

For he made a great figure in Egypt for his signal services.

For he killed the Ichneumon-rat very pernicious by land.

For his ears are so acute that they sting again.

For from this proceeds the passing quickness of his attention.

For by stroking of him I have found out electricity.

For I perceived God's light about him both wax and fire.

For the Electrical fire is the spiritual substance, which God sends from heaven to sustain the bodies both of man and beast.

For God has blessed him in the variety of his movements.

For, though he cannot fly, he is an excellent clamberer.

For his motions upon the face of the earth are more than any other
   quadrupede.
For he can tread to all the measures upon the musick.
For he can swim for life.
For he can creep.

CHRISTOPHER SMART

A Morning-piece, or, an Hymn for the Hay-makers

Brisk Chaunticleer his matins had begun,
     And broke the silence of the night,
  And thrice he called aloud the tardy sun,
     And thrice he hailed the dawn's ambiguous light;
Back to their graves the fear-begotten phantoms run.

Strong Labour got up with his pipe in his mouth,
     And stoutly strode over the dale,
  He lent new perfumes to the breath of the south,
     On his back hung his wallet and flail.
Behind him came Health from her cottage of thatch,
Where never physician had lifted the latch.

First of the village Colin was awake,
And thus he sung, reclining on his rake:
     Now the rural graces three
     Dance beneath yon maple tree;
     First the vestal Virtue, known
     By her adamantine zone;
     Next to her in rosy pride,
     Sweet Society, the bride;
     Last Honesty, full seemly dressed
     In her cleanly home-spun vest.
The abbey bells in wak'ning rounds
     The warning peal have giv'n;
And pious Gratitude resounds
     Her morning hymn to heav'n.

All nature wakes – the birds unlock their throats,
And mock the shepherd's rustic notes.
    All alive o'er the lawn,
    Full glad of the dawn,
      The little lambkins play,
Sylvia and Sol arise, – and all is day –

    Come, my mates, let us work,
    And all hands to the fork,
While the sun shines, our hay-cocks to make,
    So fine is the day,
    And so fragrant the hay,
That the meadow's as blithe as the wake.

    Our voices let's raise
    In Phoebus's praise;
Inspired by so glorious a theme,
    Our musical words
    Shall be joined by the birds,
And we'll dance to the tune of the stream.

CHRISTOPHER SMART

An Elegy on the Death of a Mad Dog

    Good people all, of every sort,
      Give ear unto my song;
    And if you find it wond'rous short,
      It cannot hold you long.

    In Islington there was a man,
      Of whom the world might say
    That still a godly race he ran,
      Whene'er he went to pray.

    A kind and gentle heart he had,
      To comfort friends and foes;
    The naked every day he clad,
      When he put on his clothes.

And in that town a dog was found,
    As many dogs there be,
Both mongrel, puppy, whelp and hound,
    And curs of low degree.

This dog and man at first were friends;
    But when a pique began,
The dog, to gain some private ends,
    Went mad and bit the man.

Around from all the neighbouring streets
    The wondering neighbours ran,
And swore the dog had lost his wits,
    To bite so good a man.

The wound it seemed both sore and sad
    To every Christian eye;
And while they swore the dog was mad,
    They swore the man would die.

But soon a wonder came to light,
    That showed the rogues they lied:
The man recovered of the bite,
    The dog it was that died.

OLIVER GOLDSMITH

from *The Deserted Village*

  Sweet Auburn! loveliest village of the plain;
Where health and plenty cheered the labouring swain,
Where smiling spring its earliest visit paid,
And parting summer's lingering blooms delayed:
Dear lovely bowers of innocence and ease,
Seats of my youth, when every sport could please,
How often have I loitered o'er thy green,
Where humble happiness endeared each scene!
How often have I paused on every charm,

The sheltered cot, the cultivated farm,
The never-failing brook, the busy mill,
The decent church that topped the neighbouring hill,
The hawthorn bush, with seats beneath the shade,
For talking age and whispering lovers made!
How often have I blest the coming day,
When toil remitting lent its turn to play,
And all the village train, from labour free,
Led up their sports beneath the spreading tree,
While many a pastime circled in the shade,
The young contending as the old surveyed;
And many a gambol frolicked o'er the ground,
And sleights of art and feats of strength went round.
And still, as each repeated pleasure tired,
Succeeding sports the mirthful band inspired;
The dancing pair that simply sought renown,
By holding out to tire each other down;
The swain mistrustless of his smutted face,
While secret laughter tittered round the place;
The bashful virgin's side-long looks of love,
The matron's glance that would those looks reprove:
These were thy charms, sweet village! sports like these,
With sweet succession, taught even toil to please:
These round thy bowers their cheerful influence shed;
These were thy charms – but all these charms are fled.

Sweet smiling village, loveliest of the lawn,
Thy sports are fled, and all thy charms withdrawn;
Amidst thy bowers the tyrant's hand is seen,
And desolation saddens all the green:
One only master grasps the whole domain,
And half a tillage stints thy smiling plain.
No more thy glassy brook reflects the day,
But, choked with sedges, works its weedy way;
Along thy glades, a solitary guest,
The hollow sounding bittern guards its nest:
Amidst thy desert walks the lapwing flies,
And tires their echoes with unvaried cries;

Sunk are thy bowers in shapeless ruin all,
And the long grass o'ertops the mouldering wall;
And trembling, shrinking from the spoiler's hand,
Far, far away thy children leave the land.

Ill fares the land, to hastening ills a prey,
Where wealth accumulates, and men decay:
Princes and lords may flourish, or may fade;
A breath can make them, as a breath has made;
But a bold peasantry, their country's pride,
When, once destroyed, can never be supplied.

A time there was, ere England's griefs began,
When every rood of ground maintained its man;
For him light labour spread her wholesome store,
Just gave what life required, but gave no more:
His blest companions, innocence and health;
And his best riches, ignorance of wealth.

But times are altered; trade's unfeeling train
Usurp the land and dispossess the swain;
Along the lawn, where scattered hamlets rose,
Unwieldy wealth and cumbrous pomp repose,
And every want to opulence allied,
And every pang that folly pays to pride.
These gentle hours that plenty bade to bloom,
Those calm desires that asked but little room,
Those healthful sports that graced the peaceful scene,
Lived in each look, and brightened all the green;
These, far departing, seek a kinder shore,
And rural mirth and manners are no more.

Sweet Auburn! parent of the blissful hour,
Thy glades forlorn confess the tyrant's power.
Here, as I take my solitary rounds
Amid thy tangling walks and ruined grounds,
And, many a year elapsed, return to view
Where once the cottage stood, the hawthorn grew,
Remembrance wakes with all her busy train,
Swells at my breast, and turns the past to pain.

Sweet was the sound, when oft at evening's close
Up yonder hill the village murmur rose.
There, as I passed with careless steps and slow,
The mingling notes came softened from below;
The swain responsive as the milk-maid sung,
The sober herd that lowed to meet their young,
The noisy geese that gabbled o'er the pool,
The playful children just let loose from school,
The watch-dog's voice that bayed the whispering wind,
And the loud laugh that spoke the vacant mind; –
These all in sweet confusion sought the shade,
And filled each pause the nightingale had made.
But now the sounds of population fail,
No cheerful murmurs fluctuate in the gale,
No busy steps the grass-grown foot-way tread,
For all the bloomy flush of life is fled.
All but yon widowed, solitary thing,
That feebly bends beside the plashy spring:
She, wretched matron, forced in age, for bread,
To strip the brook with mantling cresses spread,
To pick her wintry faggot from the thorn,
To seek her nightly shed, and weep till morn;
She only left of all the harmless train,
The sad historian of the pensive plain.

Near yonder copse, where once the garden smiled,
And still where many a garden flower grows wild;
There, where a few torn shrubs the place disclose,
The village preacher's modest mansion rose.
A man he was to all the country dear,
And passing rich with forty pounds a year;
Remote from towns he ran his godly race,
Nor e'er had changed, nor wished to change his place . . .

Beside yon straggling fence that skirts the way,
With blossomed furze unprofitably gay,
There, in his noisy mansion, skilled to rule,
The village master taught his little school.
A man severe he was, and stern to view;

I knew him well, and every truant knew;
Well had the boding tremblers learned to trace
The day's disasters in his morning face;
Full well they laughed with counterfeited glee
At all his jokes, for many a joke had he . . .

But past is all his fame. The very spot
Where many a time he triumphed, is forgot.
Near yonder thorn, that lifts its head on high,
Where once the sign-post caught the passing eye,
Low lies that house where nut-brown draughts inspired,
Where greybeard mirth and smiling toil retired,
Where village statesmen talked with looks profound,
And news much older than their ale went round.

Thither no more the peasant shall repair
To sweet oblivion of his daily care;
No more the farmer's news, the barber's tale;
No more the woodman's ballad shall prevail;
No more the smith his dusky brow shall clear,
Relax his ponderous strength, and lean to hear;
The host himself no longer shall be found
Careful to see the mantling bliss go round;
Nor the coy maid, half willing to be prest,
Shall kiss the cup to pass it to the rest.

Yes! let the rich deride, the proud disdain
These simple blessings of the lowly train;
To me more dear, congenial to my heart,
One native charm, than all the gloss of art.
Spontaneous joys, where Nature has its play,
The soul adopts, and owns their first-born sway;
Lightly they frolic o'er the vacant mind,
Unenvied, unmolested, unconfined.
But the long pomp, the midnight masquerade,
With all the freaks of wanton wealth arrayed –
In these, ere triflers half their wish obtain,
The toiling pleasure sickens into pain;
And, even while fashion's brightest arts decoy,
The heart distrusting asks if this be joy.

Ye friends to truth, ye statesmen who survey
The rich man's joy increase, the poor's decay,
'Tis yours to judge, how wide the limits stand
Between a splendid and an happy land.
Proud swells the tide with loads of freighted ore,
And shouting Folly hails them from her shore;
Hoards even beyond the miser's wish abound,
And rich men flock from all the world around.
Yet count our gains! This wealth is but a name
That leaves our useful products still the same.
Not so the loss. The man of wealth and pride
Takes up a space that many poor supplied;
Space for his lake, his park's extended bounds,
Space for his horses, equipage, and hounds:
The robe that wraps his limbs in silken sloth
Has robbed the neighbouring fields of half their growth;
His seat, where solitary sports are seen,
Indignant spurns the cottage from the green:
Around the world each needful product flies,
For all the luxuries the world supplies;
While thus the land adorned for pleasure all
In barren splendour feebly waits the fall.

OLIVER GOLDSMITH

from *The Rosciad*

[CHARACTER OF A CRITIC]

With that low cunning, which in fools supplies,
And amply too, the place of being wise,
Which nature, kind indulgent parent, gave
To qualify the blockhead for a knave;
With that smooth falsehood, whose appearance charms,
And reason of each wholesome doubt disarms,
Which to the lowest depths of guile descends,
By vilest means pursues the vilest ends,
Wears friendship's mask for purposes of spite,

Fawns in the day, and butchers in the night;
With that malignant envy, which turns pale
And sickens, even if a friend prevail,
Which merit and success pursues with hate,
And damns the worth it cannot imitate;
With the cold caution of a coward's spleen,
Which fears not guilt, but always seeks a screen,
Which keeps this maxim ever in her view –
What's basely done, should be done safely too;
With that dull, rooted, callous impudence,
Which, dead to shame and ev'ry nicer sense,
Ne'er blushed, unless, in spreading vice's snares,
She blundered on some virtue unawares;
With all these blessings, which we seldom find
Lavished by nature on one happy mind,
A motley figure, of the Fribble tribe,
Which heart can scarce conceive, or pen describe,
Came simp'ring on; to ascertain whose sex
Twelve sage impannelled matrons would perplex.
Nor male, nor female; neither, and yet both;
Of neuter gender, though of Irish growth;
A six-foot suckling, mincing in his gait,
Affected, peevish, prim and delicate;
Fearful it seemed, though of athletic make,
Lest brutal breezes should too roughly shake
Its tender form, and savage motion spread
O'er its pale cheeks the horrid manly red.

　　Much did it talk in its own pretty phrase,
Of genius and of taste, of play'rs and plays;
Much too of writings, which itself had wrote,
Of special merit, though of little note,
For fate, in a strange humour, had decreed
That what it wrote, none but itself should read;
Much too it chattered of dramatic laws,
Misjudging critics, and misplaced applause,
Then, with a self-complacent jutting air,
It smiled, it smirked, it wriggled to the chair;
And with an awkward briskness not his own,

Looking around, and perking on the throne,
Triumphant seemed; when that strange savage dame,
Known but to few, or only known by name,
Plain Common Sense appeared, by nature there
Appointed, with plain truth, to guard the chair.
The pageant saw and, blasted with her frown,
To its first state of nothing melted down.

Nor shall the Muse (for even there the pride
Of this vain nothing shall be mortified)
Nor shall the Muse (should fate ordain her rhymes,
Fond pleasing thought! to live in aftertimes)
With such a trifler's name her pages blot;
Known be the character, the thing forgot;
Let it, to disappoint each future aim,
Live without sex, and die without a name!

CHARLES CHURCHILL

Song

Here's to the maiden of bashful fifteen;
    Here's to the widow of fifty;
Here's to the flaunting, extravagant quean,
    And here's to the housewife that's thrifty.
        Chorus. Let the toast pass, –
        Drink to the lass,
I'll warrant she'll prove an excuse for the glass.

Here's to the charmer whose dimples we prize;
    Now to the maid who has none, sir:
Here's to the girl with a pair of blue eyes,
    And here's to the nymph with but *one*, sir.
        Chorus. Let the toast pass, &c.

Here's to the maid with a bosom of snow,
    Now to her that's as brown as a berry:
Here's to the wife with a face full of woe,
    And now for the damsel that's merry.
        Chorus. Let the toast pass, &c.

58

For let 'em be clumsy, or let 'em be slim,
   Young or ancient, I care not a feather;
So fill a pint-bumper quite up to the brim,
   And let us e'en toast 'em together.
    Chorus. Let the toast pass, &c.

RICHARD BRINSLEY SHERIDAN

Ode on a Distant Prospect of Eton College

Ye distant spires, ye antique towers
   That crown the watery glade,
Where grateful Science still adores
   Her Henry's holy shade;
And ye, that from the stately brow
Of Windsor's heights th' expanse below
Of grove, of lawn, of mead survey,
Whose turf, whose shade, whose flowers among
Wanders the hoary Thames along
   His silver-winding way:

Ah happy hills! ah pleasing shade!
   Ah fields beloved in vain!
Where once my careless childhood stray'd,
   A stranger yet to pain!
I feel the gales that from ye blow
A momentary bliss bestow,
As waving fresh their gladsome wing
My weary soul they seem to soothe,
And, redolent of joy and youth,
   To breathe a second spring.

Say, Father Thames, for thou hast seen
   Full many a sprightly race
Disporting on thy margent green
   The paths of pleasure trace;
Who foremost now delight to cleave
With pliant arm, thy glassy wave?

The captive linnet which enthral?
What idle progeny succeed
To chase the rolling circle's speed
    Or urge the flying ball?

While some on earnest business bent
    Their murmuring labours ply
'Gainst graver hours that bring constraint
    To sweeten liberty:
Some bold adventurers disdain
The limits of their little reign
And unknown regions dare descry:
Still as they run they look behind,
They hear a voice in every wind,
    And snatch a fearful joy.

Gay hope is theirs by fancy fed,
    Less pleasing when possessed
The tear forgot as soon as shed,
    The sunshine of the breast:
Theirs buxom health, of rosy hue,
Wild wit, invention ever new,
And lively cheer, of vigour born;
The thoughtless day, the easy night,
The spirits pure, the slumbers light
    That fly th' approach of morn.

Alas! regardless of their doom
    The little victims play;
No sense have they of ills to come
    Nor care beyond to-day:
Yet see how all around 'em wait
The ministers of human fate
And black Misfortune's baleful train!
Ah show them where in ambush stand
To seize their prey, the murderous band!
    Ah, tell them they are men!

These shall the fury Passions tear,
    The vultures of the mind,

Disdainful Anger, pallid Fear,
    And Shame that sculks behind;
Or pining Love shall waste their youth,
Or Jealousy with rankling tooth
That inly gnaws the secret heart,
And Envy wan, and faded Care,
Grim-visaged comfortless Despair,
    And Sorrow's piercing dart.

Ambition this shall tempt to rise,
    Then whirl the wretch from high
To bitter Scorn a sacrifice
    And grinning Infamy.
The stings of Falsehood those shall try
And hard Unkindness' alter'd eye,
That mocks the tear it forced to flow;
And keen Remorse with blood defiled,
And moody Madness laughing wild
    Amid severest woe.

Lo, in the vale of years beneath
    A grisly troop are seen,
The painful family of Death,
    More hideous than their queen:
This racks the joints, this fires the veins,
That every labouring sinew strains,
Those in the deeper vitals rage:
Lo! Poverty, to fill the band,
That numbs the soul with icy hand,
    And slow-consuming Age.

To each his sufferings: all are men,
    Condemn'd alike to groan;
The tender for another's pain,
    Th' unfeeling for his own.
Yet, ah! why should they know their fate,
Since sorrow never comes too late,
And happiness too swiftly flies?
Thought would destroy their paradise.

No more; – where ignorance is bliss,
'Tis folly to be wise.

THOMAS GRAY

The Lady Who Offers Her Looking-glass to Venus

Venus, take my votive glass:
Since I am not what I was,
What from this day I shall be,
Venus, let me never see.

MATTHEW PRIOR

The Bard

PINDARIC ODE

'Ruin seize thee, ruthless King!
   Confusion on thy banners wait;
Tho' fann'd by Conquest's crimson wing
   They mock the air with idle state.
Helm, nor hauberk's twisted mail,
Nor e'en thy virtues, Tyrant, shall avail
To save thy secret soul from nightly fears,
From Cambria's curse, from Cambria's tears!'
– Such were the sounds that o'er the crested pride
Of the first Edward scatter'd wild dismay,
As down the steep of Snowdon's shaggy side
   He wound with toilsome march his long array: –
Stout Glo'ster stood aghast in speechless trance;
'To arms!' cried Mortimer, and couch'd his quivering lance.

   On a rock, whose haughty brow
Frowns o'er old Conway's foaming flood,
   Robed in the sable garb of woe
With haggard eyes the Poet stood:

62

(Loose his beard and hoary hair
Stream'd like a meteor to the troubled air)
And with a master's hand and prophet's fire
Struck the deep sorrows of his lyre:
    'Hark, how each giant-oak and desert-cave
Sighs to the torrent's awful voice beneath!
O'er thee, oh King! their hundred arms they wave,
    Revenge on thee in hoarser murmurs breathe;
Vocal no more, since Cambria's fatal day,
To high-born Hoel's harp, or soft Llewellyn's lay.

'Cold is Cadwallo's tongue,
That hush'd the stormy main:
Brave Urien sleeps upon his craggy bed:
    Mountains, ye mourn in vain
    Modred, whose magic song
Made huge Plinlimmon bow his cloud-topt head.
    On dreary Arvon's shore they lie
Smear'd with gore and ghastly pale:
Far, far aloof the affrighted ravens sail;
    The famish'd eagle screams, and passes by.
Dear lost companions of my tuneful art,
    Dear as the light that visits these sad eyes,
Dear as the ruddy drops that warm my heart,
    Ye died amidst your dying country's cries –
No more I weep; They do not sleep;
    On yonder cliffs, a grisly band,
I see them sit; They linger yet,
    Avengers of their native land:
With me in dreadful harmony they join,
And weave with bloody hands the tissue of thy line.

'Weave the warp and weave the woof
    The winding sheet of Edward's race:
    Give ample room and verge enough
    The characters of hell to trace.
Mark the year, and mark the night,
When Severn shall re-echo with affright
The shrieks of death thro' Berkley's roof that ring,

Shrieks of an agonizing king!
    She-wolf of France, with unrelenting fangs
That tear'st the bowels of thy mangled mate,
    From thee be born, who o'er thy country hangs
The scourge of heaven. What terrors round him wait!
Amazement in his van, with flight combined,
And sorrow's faded form, and solitude behind.

'Mighty victor, mighty lord,
    Low on his funeral couch he lies!
No pitying heart, no eye, afford
    A tear to grace his obsequies.
Is the sable warrior fled?
Thy son is gone. He rests among the dead.
The swarm that in thy noon-tide beam were born?
– Gone to salute the rising morn.
Fair laughs the Morn, and soft the zephyr blows,
    While proudly riding o'er the azure realm
In gallant trim the gilded vessel goes:
    Youth on the prow, and Pleasure at the helm:
Regardless of the sweeping whirlwind's sway,
That hush'd in grim repose expects his evening prey.

'Fill high the sparkling bowl,
The rich repast prepare;
    Reft of a crown, he yet may share the feast:
Close by the regal chair
    Fell Thirst and Famine scowl
    A baleful smile upon their baffled guest.
Heard ye the din of battle bray,
    Lance to lance, and horse to horse?
    Long years of havock urge their destined course,
And thro' the kindred squadrons mow their way.

'Ye towers of Julius, London's lasting shame,
With many a foul and midnight murder fed,
    Revere his consort's faith, his father's fame,
And spare the meek usurper's holy head!
Above, below, the rose of snow,

Twined with her blushing foe, we spread:
The bristled boar in infant-gore
   Wallows beneath the thorny shade.
Now, brothers, bending o'er the accursèd loom,
Stamp we our vengeance deep, and ratify his doom.

'*Edward, lo! to sudden fate*
   (Weave we the woof; The thread is spun;)
Half of thy heart we consecrate.
   (The web is wove; The work is done.)
—Stay, oh stay! nor thus forlorn
Leave me unbless'd, unpitied, here to mourn:
In yon bright track that fires the western skies
They melt, they vanish from my eyes.
But oh! what solemn scenes on Snowdon's height
   Descending slow their glittering skirts unroll?
Visions of glory, spare my aching sight,
Ye unborn ages, crowd not on my soul!
No more our long-lost Arthur we bewail: —
All hail, ye genuine kings! Britannia's issue, hail!

   Girt with many a baron bold
Sublime their starry fronts they rear;
   And gorgeous dames, and statesmen old
In bearded majesty, appear.
In the midst a form divine!
Her eye proclaims her of the Briton-line:
Her lion-port, her awe-commanding face
Attemper'd sweet to virgin-grace.
What strings symphonious tremble in the air,
   What strains of vocal transport round her play?
Hear from the grave, great Taliessin, hear;
   They breathe a soul to animate thy clay.
Bright Rapture calls, and soaring as she sings,
Waves in the eye of heaven her many-colour'd wings.

The verse adorn again
   Fierce war, and faithful love,
And truth severe, by fairy fiction drest.
   In buskin'd measures move

Pale grief, and pleasing pain,
With horror, tyrant of the throbbing breast.
A voice as of the cherub-choir
   Gales from blooming Eden bear,
   And distant warblings lessen on my ear
That lost in long futurity expire.
Fond impious man, think'st thou yon sanguine cloud
   Raised by thy breath, has quench'd the orb of day?
To-morrow he repairs the golden flood
   And warms the nations with redoubled ray.
Enough for me: with joy I see
   The different doom our fates assign:
Be thine despair and sceptred care,
   To triumph and to die are mine.'
– He spoke, and headlong from the mountain's height
Deep in the roaring tide he plunged to endless night.

THOMAS GRAY

An Epitaph Intended for Sir Isaac Newton in Westminster Abbey

ISAACUS NEWTONUS:
QUEM IMMORTALEM
TESTANTUR TEMPUS, NATURA, COELUM:
MORTALEM
HOC MARMOR FATETUR.

Nature and Nature's laws lay hid in night:
God said, Let Newton be! and all was light.

ALEXANDER POPE

Light Shining out of Darkness

God moves in a mysterious way,
    His wonders to perform;
He plants his footsteps in the sea,
    And rides upon the storm.

Deep in unfathomable mines
    Of never-failing skill,
He treasures up his bright designs,
    And works his sovereign will.

Ye fearful saints fresh courage take,
    The clouds ye so much dread
Are big with mercy, and shall break
    In blessings on your head.

Judge not the Lord by feeble sense,
    But trust him for his grace;
Behind a frowning providence,
    He hides a smiling face.

His purposes will ripen fast,
    Unfolding ev'ry hour;
The bud may have a bitter taste,
    But sweet will be the flow'r.

Blind unbelief is sure to err,
    And scan his work in vain;
God is his own interpreter,
    And he will make it plain.

WILLIAM COWPER

Hymn to the Nativity of Our Lord and Saviour Jesus Christ

Where is this stupendous stranger,
    Swains of Solyma, advise;
Lead me to my Master's manger,
    Show me where my Saviour lies.

O most Mighty! O most Holy!
    Far beyond the seraph's thought,
Art thou then so mean and lowly
    As unheeded prophets taught?

O the magnitude of meekness!
    Worth from worth immortal sprung;
O the strength of infant weakness,
    If eternal is so young!

If so young and thus eternal,
    Michael tune the shepherd's reed,
Where the scenes are ever vernal,
    And the loves be love indeed!

See the God blasphemed and doubted
    In the schools of Greece and Rome;
See the pow'rs of darkness routed,
    Taken at their utmost gloom.

Nature's decorations glisten
    Far above their usual trim;
Birds on box and laurels listen,
    As so near the cherubs hymn.

Boreas now no longer winters
    On the desolated coast;
Oaks no more are riv'n in splinters
    By the whirlwind and his host.

Spinks and ouzels sing sublimely,
    'We too have a Saviour born';
Whiter blossoms burst untimely
    On the blest Mosaic thorn.

God all-bounteous, all-creative,
    Whom no ills from good dissuade,
Is incarnate, and a native
    Of the very world he made.

CHRISTOPHER SMART

from *The Traveller, or A Prospect of Society*

[BRITAIN]

Creation's mildest charms are there combined,
Extremes are only in the master's mind.
Stern o'er each bosom reason holds her state,
With daring aims irregularly great;
Pride in their port, defiance in their eye,
I see the lords of human kind pass by,
Intent on high designs, a thoughtful band,
By forms unfashioned, fresh from nature's hand;
Fierce in their native hardiness of soul,
True to imagined right, above control,
While even the peasant boasts these rights to scan,
And learns to venerate himself as man.

    Thine, Freedom, thine the blessings pictured here,
Thine are those charms that dazzle and endear;
Too blest, indeed, were such without alloy,
But fostered even by Freedom, ills annoy:
That independence Britons prize too high,
Keeps man from man and breaks the social tie;
The self-dependent lordlings stand alone,
All claims that bind and sweeten life unknown;
Here by the bonds of nature feebly held,
Minds combat minds, repelling and repelled.
Ferments arise, imprisoned factions roar,
Repressed ambition struggles round her shore,
Till over-wrought, the general system feels
Its motions stopped, or frenzy fire the wheels.

    Nor this the worst. As nature's ties decay,
As duty, love and honour fail to sway,
Fictitious bonds, the bonds of wealth and law,
Still gather strength and force unwilling awe.
Hence all obedience bows to these alone,
And talent sinks and merit weeps unknown;

Till time may come when, stripped of all her charms,
The land of scholars and the nurse of arms,
Where noble stems transmit the patriot flame,
Where kings have toiled and poets wrote for fame,
One sink of level avarice shall lie,
And scholars, soldiers, kings unhonoured die.

OLIVER GOLDSMITH

How Small, of All That Human Hearts Endure

How small, of all that human hearts endure,
That part which laws or kings can cause or cure.
Still to ourselves in every place consign'd,
Our own felicity we make or find;
With secret course, which no loud storms annoy,
Glides the smooth current of domestic joy.
[The lifted ax, the agonizing wheel,
Luke's iron crown, and Damien's bed of steel,]
To men remote from power but rarely known,
Leave reason, faith, and conscience all our own.

SAMUEL JOHNSON

The Poplar-field

The poplars are felled, farewell to the shade
And the whispering sound of the cool colonnade,
The winds play no longer, and sing in the leaves,
Nor Ouse on his bosom their image receives.

Twelve years have elapsed since I last took a view
Of my favourite field and the bank where they grew,
And now in the grass behold they are laid,
And the tree is my seat that once lent me a shade.

The blackbird has fled to another retreat
Where the hazels afford him a screen from the heat,
And the scene where his melody charmed me before,
Resounds with his sweet-flowing ditty no more.

My fugitive years are all hasting away,
And I must ere long lie as lowly as they,
With a turf on my breast, and a stone at my head,
Ere another such grove shall arise in its stead.

'Tis a sight to engage me, if any thing can,
To muse on the perishing pleasures of man;
Though his life be a dream, his enjoyments, I see,
Have a being less durable even than he.

WILLIAM COWPER

Epitaph on a Hare

Here lies, whom hound did ne'er pursue,
    Nor swifter greyhound follow,
Whose foot ne'er tainted morning dew,
    Nor ear heard huntsman's 'hallo',

Old Tiney, surliest of his kind,
    Who, nursed with tender care,
And to domestic bounds confined,
    Was still a wild jack-hare.

Though duly from my hand he took
    His pittance ev'ry night,
He did it with a jealous look,
    And, when he could, would bite.

His diet was of wheaten bread,
    And milk, and oats, and straw,
Thistles, or lettuces instead,
    With sand to scour his maw.

On twigs of hawthorn he regaled,
    On pippins' russet peel;
And, when his juicy salads failed,
    Sliced carrot pleased him well.

A Turkey carpet was his lawn,
    Whereon he loved to bound,
To skip and gambol like a fawn,
    And swing his rump around.

His frisking was at evening hours,
    For then he lost his fear;
But most before approaching show'rs,
    Or when a storm drew near.

Eight years and five round-rolling moons
    He thus saw steal away,
Dozing out all his idle noons,
    And ev'ry night at play.

I kept him for his humour's sake,
    For he would oft beguile
My heart of thoughts that made it ache,
    And force me to a smile.

But now, beneath this walnut-shade
    He finds his long, last home,
And waits in snug concealment laid,
    Till gentler Puss shall come.

He, still more agèd, feels the shocks
    From which no care can save,
And, partner once of Tiney's box,
    Must soon partake his grave.

WILLIAM COWPER

from *The Castaway*

Obscurest night involved the sky,
   Th' Atlantic billows roared,
When such a destined wretch as I,
   Washed headlong from on board,
Of friends, of hope, of all bereft,
His floating home for ever left.

No braver chief could Albion boast
   Than he with whom he went,
Nor ever ship left Albion's coast
   With warmer wishes sent.

No poet wept him: but the page
   Of narrative sincere,
That tells his name, his worth, his age,
   Is wet with Anson's tear.
And tears by bards or heroes shed
Alike immortalize the dead.

I therefore purpose not or dream,
   Descanting on his fate,
To give the melancholy theme
   A more enduring date:
But misery still delights to trace
Its semblance in another's case.

No voice divine the storm allayed,
   No light propitious shone,
When, snatched from all effectual aid,
   We perished, each alone:
But I beneath a rougher sea,
And whelmed in deeper gulfs than he.

WILLIAM COWPER

Verses, Supposed to be Written by Alexander Selkirk, During his Solitary Abode in the Island of Juan Fernandez

I am monarch of all I survey,
    My right there is none to dispute;
From the centre all round to the sea,
    I am lord of the fowl and the brute.
Oh, solitude! where are the charms
    That sages have seen in thy face?
Better dwell in the midst of alarms,
    Than reign in this horrible place.

I am out of humanity's reach,
    I must finish my journey alone,
Never hear the sweet music of speech;
    I start at the sound of my own.
The beasts, that roam over the plain,
    My form with indifference see;
They are so unacquainted with man,
    Their tameness is shocking to me.

Society, friendship, and love,
    Divinely bestowed upon man,
Oh, had I the wings of a dove,
    How soon would I taste you again!
My sorrows I then might assuage
    In the ways of religion and truth,
Might learn from the wisdom of age,
    And be cheered by the sallies of youth.

Religion! what treasure untold
    Resides in that heavenly word!
More precious than silver and gold,
    Or all that this earth can afford.
But the sound of the church-going bell
    These valleys and rocks never heard,
Ne'er sighed at the sound of a knell,
    Or smiled when a sabbath appeared.

Ye winds, that have made me your sport,
    Convey to this desolate shore
Some cordial endearing report
    Of a land I shall visit no more.
My friends, do they now and then send
    A wish or a thought after me?
O tell me I yet have a friend,
    Though a friend I am never to see.

How fleet is a glance of the mind!
    Compared with the speed of its flight,
The tempest itself lags behind,
    And the swift-winged arrows of light.
When I think of my own native land,
    In a moment I seem to be there;
But alas! recollection at hand
    Soon hurries me back to despair.

But the sea-fowl is gone to her nest,
    The beast is laid down in his lair,
Ev'n here is a season of rest,
    And I to my cabin repair.
There is mercy in every place;
    And mercy, encouraging thought!
Gives even affliction a grace,
    And reconciles man to his lot.

WILLIAM COWPER

The Vanity of Human Wishes

THE TENTH SATIRE OF JUVENAL IMITATED

Let observation with extensive view
Survey mankind from China to Peru;
Remark each anxious toil, each eager strife,
And watch the busy scenes of crowded life;
Then say how hope and fear, desire and hate,
O'erspread with snares the clouded maze of fate,

Where wav'ring man, betrayed by vent'rous pride
To tread the dreary paths without a guide,
As treach'rous phantoms in the mist delude,
Shuns fancied ills, or chases airy good.
How rarely reason guides the stubborn choice,
Rules the bold hand, or prompts the suppliant voice;
How nations sink, by darling schemes oppressed,
When vengeance listens to the fool's request.
Fate wings with ev'ry wish th' afflictive dart,
Each gift of nature, and each grace of art;
With fatal heat impetuous courage glows,
With fatal sweetness elocution flows,
Impeachment stops the speaker's pow'rful breath,
And restless fire precipitates on death.

    But scarce observed, the knowing and the bold
Fall in the gen'ral massacre of gold;
Wide-wasting pest! that rages unconfined,
And crowds with crimes the records of mankind;
For gold his sword the hireling ruffian draws,
For gold the hireling judge distorts the laws;
Wealth heaped on wealth nor truth nor safety buys,
The dangers gather as the treasures rise.

    Let hist'ry tell where rival kings command,
And dubious title shakes the madded land,
When statutes glean the refuse of the sword,
How much more safe the vassal than the lord;
Low skulks the hind beneath the rage of pow'r,
And leaves the wealthy traitor in the Tow'r,
Untouched his cottage, and his slumbers sound,
Though confiscation's vultures hover round.

    The needy traveller, serene and gay,
Walks the wild heath, and sings his toil away.
Does envy seize thee? crush th' upbraiding joy,
Increase his riches and his peace destroy;
Now fears in dire vicissitude invade,
The rustling brake alarms, and quiv'ring shade,
Nor light nor darkness bring his pain relief,
One shows the plunder, and one hides the thief.

Yet still one gen'ral cry the skies assails,
And gain and grandeur load the tainted gales;
Few know the toiling statesman's fear or care,
Th' insidious rival and the gaping heir.

Once more, Democritus, arise on earth,
With cheerful wisdom and instructive mirth,
See motley life in modern trappings dressed,
And feed with varied fools th' eternal jest:
Thou who couldst laugh where want enchained caprice,
Toil crushed conceit, and man was of a piece;
Where wealth unloved without a mourner died;
And scarce a sycophant was fed by pride;
Where ne'er was known the form of mock debate,
Or seen a new-made mayor's unwieldy state;
Where change of fav'rites made no change of laws,
And senates heard before they judged a cause;
How wouldst thou shake at Britain's modish tribe,
Dart the quick taunt, and edge the piercing gibe?
Attentive truth and nature to descry,
And pierce each scene with philosophic eye.
To thee were solemn toys or empty show,
The robes of pleasure and the veils of woe:
All aid the farce, and all thy mirth maintain,
Whose joys are causeless, or whose griefs are vain.

Such was the scorn that filled the sage's mind,
Renewed at ev'ry glance on humankind;
How just that scorn ere yet thy voice declare,
Search every state, and canvass ev'ry pray'r.

Unnumbered suppliants crowd preferment's gate,
Athirst for wealth, and burning to be great;
Delusive Fortune hears th' incessant call,
They mount, they shine, evaporate and fall.
On ev'ry stage the foes of peace attend,
Hate dogs their flight, and insult mocks their end.
Love ends with hope, the sinking statesman's door
Pours in the morning worshipper no more;
For growing names the weekly scribbler lies,
To growing wealth the dedicator flies,

From every room descends the painted face,
That hung the bright Palladium of the place,
And smoked in kitchens, or in auctions sold,
To better features yields the frame of gold;
For now no more we trace in ev'ry line
Heroic worth, benevolence divine:
The form distorted justifies the fall,
And detestation rids th' indignant wall.

But will not Britain hear the last appeal,
Sign her foes' doom, or guard her fav'rites' zeal?
Through Freedom's sons no more remonstrance rings,
Degrading nobles and controlling kings;
Our supple tribes repress their patriot throats,
And ask no questions but the price of votes;
With weekly libels and septennial ale,
Their wish is full to riot and to rail.

In full-blown dignity, see Wolsey stand,
Law in his voice, and fortune in his hand:
To him the church, the realm, their pow'rs consign,
Through him the rays of regal bounty shine,
Turned by his nod the stream of honour flows,
His smile alone security bestows:
Still to new heights his restless wishes tow'r,
Claim leads to claim, and pow'r advances pow'r;
Till conquest unresisted ceased to please,
And rights submitted left him none to seize.
At length his sov'reign frowns – the train of state
Mark the keen glance, and watch the sign to hate.
Where'er he turns he meets a stranger's eye,
His suppliants scorn him, and his followers fly;
At once is lost the pride of awful state,
The golden canopy, the glitt'ring plate,
The regal palace, the luxurious board,
The liv'ried army, and the menial lord.
With age, with cares, with maladies oppressed,
He seeks the refuge of monastic rest.
Grief aids disease, remembered folly stings,
And his last sighs reproach the faith of kings.

Speak thou, whose thoughts at humble peace repine,
Shall Wolsey's wealth, with Wolsey's end be thine?
Or liv'st thou now, with safer pride content,
The wisest justice on the banks of Trent?
For why did Wolsey, near the steeps of fate,
On weak foundations raise th' enormous weight?
Why but to sink beneath misfortune's blow,
With louder ruin to the gulfs below?

  What gave great Villiers to th' assassin's knife,
And fixed disease on Harley's closing life?
What murdered Wentworth, and what exiled Hyde,
By kings protected and to kings allied?
What but their wish indulged in courts to shine,
And pow'r too great to keep, or to resign?

  When first the college rolls receive his name,
The young enthusiast quits his ease for fame;
Through all his veins the fever of renown
Burns from the strong contagion of the gown;
O'er Bodley's dome his future labours spread,
And Bacon's mansion trembles o'er his head.
Are these thy views? proceed, illustrious youth,
And virtue guard thee to the throne of truth!
Yet should thy soul indulge the gen'rous heat,
Till captive Science yields her last retreat;
Should Reason guide thee with her brightest ray,
And pour on misty doubt resistless day;
Should no false kindness lure to loose delight,
Nor praise relax, nor difficulty fright;
Should tempting Novelty thy cell refrain,
And Sloth effuse her opiate fumes in vain;
Should Beauty blunt on fops her fatal dart,
Nor claim the triumph of a lettered heart;
Should no disease thy torpid veins invade,
Nor Melancholy's phantoms haunt thy shade;
Yet hope not life from grief or danger free,
Nor think the doom of man reversed for thee:
Deign on the passing world to turn thine eyes,
And pause awhile from letters to be wise;

There mark what ills the scholar's life assail,
Toil, envy, want, the patron, and the jail.
See nations slowly wise, and meanly just,
To buried merit raise the tardy bust.
If dreams yet flatter, once again attend,
Hear Lydiat's life, and Galileo's end.

Nor deem, when Learning her last prize bestows,
The glitt'ring eminence exempt from foes;
See when the vulgar 'scape, despised or awed,
Rebellion's vengeful talons seize on Laud.
From meaner minds though smaller fines content,
The plundered palace or sequestered rent;
Marked out by dangerous parts he meets the shock,
And fatal Learning leads him to the block:
Around his tomb let Art and Genius weep,
But hear his death, ye blockheads, hear and sleep.

The festal blazes, the triumphal show,
The ravished standard, and the captive foe,
The senate's thanks, the gazette's pompous tale,
With force resistless o'er the brave prevail.
Such bribes the rapid Greek o'er Asia whirled,
For such the steady Romans shook the world;
For such in distant lands the Britons shine,
And stain with blood the Danube or the Rhine;
This pow'r has praise, that virtue scarce can warm,
Till fame supplies the universal charm.
Yet Reason frowns on war's unequal game,
Where wasted nations raise a single name,
And mortgaged states their grandsires' wreaths regret,
From age to age in everlasting debt;
Wreaths which at last the dear-bought right convey
To rust on medals, or on stones decay.

On what foundation stands the warrior's pride?
How just his hopes let Swedish Charles decide;
A frame of adamant, a soul of fire,
No dangers fright him, and no labours tire;
O'er love, o'er fear, extends his wide domain,
Unconquered lord of pleasure and of pain;

No joys to him pacific sceptres yield,
War sounds the trump, he rushes to the field;
Behold surrounding kings their pow'r combine,
And one capitulate, and one resign;
Peace courts his hand, but spreads her charms in vain;
'Think nothing gained,' he cries, 'till naught remain,
On Moscow's walls till Gothic standards fly,
And all be mine beneath the polar sky.'
The march begins in military state,
And nations on his eye suspended wait;
Stern Famine guards the solitary coast,
And Winter barricades the realms of frost;
He comes, not want and cold his course delay; –
Hide, blushing Glory, hide Pultowa's day:
The vanquished hero leaves his broken bands,
And shows his miseries in distant lands;
Condemned a needy supplicant to wait,
While ladies interpose, and slaves debate.
But did not Chance at length her error mend?
Did no subverted empire mark his end?
Did rival monarchs give the fatal wound?
Or hostile millions press him to the ground?
His fall was destined to a barren strand,
A petty fortress, and a dubious hand;
He left the name, at which the world grew pale,
To point a moral, or adorn a tale.

    All times their scenes of pompous woes afford,
From Persia's tyrant to Bavaria's lord.
In gay hostility, and barbarous pride,
With half mankind embattled at his side,
Great Xerxes comes to seize the certain prey,
And starves exhausted regions in his way;
Attendant Flatt'ry counts his myriads o'er,
Till counted myriads soothe his pride no more;
Fresh praise is tried till madness fires his mind,
The waves he lashes, and enchains the wind;
New pow'rs are claimed, new pow'rs are still bestowed,
Till rude resistance lops the spreading god;

The daring Greeks deride the martial show,
And heap their valleys with the gaudy foe;
Th' insulted sea with humbler thoughts he gains,
A single skiff to speed his flight remains;
Th' incumbered oar scarce leaves the dreaded coast
Through purple billows and a floating host.

    The bold Bavarian, in a luckless hour,
Tries the dread summits of Caesarian power,
With unexpected legions bursts away,
And sees defenceless realms receive his sway;
Short sway! fair Austria spreads her mournful charms,
The queen, the beauty, sets the world in arms;
From hill to hill the beacon's rousing blaze
Spreads wide the hope of plunder and of praise;
The fierce Croatian, and the wild Hussar,
With all the sons of ravage crowd the war;
The baffled prince in honour's flatt'ring bloom
Of hasty greatness finds the fatal doom,
His foes' derision, and his subjects' blame,
And steals to death from anguish and from shame.

    'Enlarge my life with multitude of days,
In health, in sickness,' thus the suppliant prays;
Hides from himself his state, and shuns to know
That life protracted is protracted woe.
Time hovers o'er, impatient to destroy,
And shuts up all the passages of joy:
In vain their gifts the bounteous seasons pour,
The fruit autumnal, and the vernal flow'r,
With listless eyes the dotard views the store,
He views, and wonders that they please no more;
Now pall the tasteless meats, and joyless wines,
And Luxury with sighs her slave resigns.
Approach, ye minstrels, try the soothing strain,
Diffuse the tuneful lenitives of pain:
No sounds, alas, would touch th' impervious ear,
Though dancing mountains witnessed Orpheus near;
Nor lute nor lyre his feeble pow'rs attend,
Nor sweeter music of a virtuous friend,

But everlasting dictates crowd his tongue,
Perversely grave, or positively wrong.
The still-returning tale, and ling'ring jest,
Perplex the fawning niece and pampered guest,
While growing hopes scarce awe the gath'ring sneer,
And scarce a legacy can bribe to hear;
The watchful guests still hint the last offence,
The daughter's petulance, the son's expense,
Improve his heady rage with treach'rous skill,
And mould his passions till they make his will.

   Unnumbered maladies his joints invade,
Lay siege to life and press the dire blockade;
But unextinguished av'rice still remains,
And dreaded losses aggravate his pains;
He turns, with anxious heart and crippled hands,
His bonds of debt, and mortgages of lands;
Or views his coffers with suspicious eyes,
Unlocks his gold, and counts it till he dies.

   But grant, the virtues of a temp'rate prime
Bless with an age exempt from scorn or crime;
An age that melts with unperceived decay,
And glides in modest innocence away;
Whose peaceful day benevolence endears,
Whose night congratulating conscience cheers;
The gen'ral fav'rite as the gen'ral friend:
Such age there is, and who shall wish its end?

   Yet ev'n on this her load Misfortune flings,
To press the weary minutes' flagging wings:
New sorrow rises as the day returns,
A sister sickens, or a daughter mourns.
Now kindred merit fills the sable bier,
Now lacerated friendship claims a tear.
Year chases year, decay pursues decay,
Still drops some joy from with'ring life away;
New forms arise, and diff'rent views engage,
Superfluous lags the vet'ran on the stage,
Till pitying Nature signs the last release,
And bids afflicted worth retire to peace.

But few there are whom hours like these await,
Who set unclouded in the gulfs of fate.
From Lydia's monarch should the search descend,
By Solon cautioned to regard his end,
In life's last scene what prodigies surprise,
Fears of the brave, and follies of the wise?
From Marlb'rough's eyes the streams of dotage flow,
And Swift expires a driv'ler and a show.

    The teeming mother, anxious for her race,
Begs for each birth the fortune of a face:
Yet Vane could tell what ills from beauty spring,
And Sedley cursed the form that pleased a king.
Ye nymphs of rosy lips and radiant eyes,
Whom pleasure keeps too busy to be wise,
Whom joys with soft varieties invite,
By day the frolic, and the dance by night,
Who frown with vanity, who smile with art,
And ask the latest fashion of the heart,
What care, what rules your heedless charms shall save,
Each nymph your rival, and each youth your slave?
Against your fame with fondness hate combines,
The rival batters, and the lover mines.
With distant voice neglected Virtue calls,
Less heard and less, the faint remonstrance falls;
Tired with contempt, she quits the slipp'ry reign,
And Pride and Prudence take her seat in vain.
In crowd at once, where none the pass defend,
The harmless freedom, and the private friend.
The guardians yield, by force superior plied;
By Int'rest, Prudence; and by Flatt'ry, Pride.
Now Beauty falls betrayed, despised, distressed,
And hissing Infamy proclaims the rest.

    Where then shall hope and fear their objects find?
Must dull suspense corrupt the stagnant mind?
Must helpless man, in ignorance sedate,
Roll darkling down the torrent of his fate?
Must no dislike alarm, no wishes rise,
No cries attempt the mercies of the skies?

Enquirer, cease, petitions yet remain,
Which heav'n may hear, nor deem religion vain.
Still raise for good the supplicating voice,
But leave to heav'n the measure and the choice,
Safe in his pow'r, whose eyes discern afar
The secret ambush of a specious pray'r.
Implore his aid, in his decisions rest,
Secure whate'er he gives, he gives the best.
Yet when the sense of sacred presence fires,
And strong devotion to the skies aspires,
Pour forth thy fervours for a healthful mind,
Obedient passions, and a will resigned;
For love, which scarce collective man can fill;
For patience sov'reign o'er transmuted ill;
For faith, that panting for a happier seat,
Counts death kind Nature's signal of retreat:
These goods for man the laws of heav'n ordain,
These goods he grants, who grants the pow'r to gain;
With these celestial wisdom calms the mind,
And makes the happiness she does not find.

SAMUEL JOHNSON

Winter

  See! Winter comes to rule the varied year,
Sullen and sad, with all his varied train,
Vapours, and clouds, and storms: be these my theme,
These, that exalt the soul to solemn thought,
And heavenly musing. Welcome, kindred glooms!
Wished, wintry horrors, hail! With frequent foot,
Pleased have I, in my cheerful morn of life,
When nursed by careless Solitude I lived,
And sung of nature with unceasing joy,
Pleased have I wandered through your rough domains;
Trod the pure, virgin snows, myself as pure,

Heard the winds roar, and the big torrent burst,
Or seen the deep, fermenting tempest brewed
In the red evening sky. Thus passed the time,
Till, through the opening chambers of the south,
Looked out the joyous Spring, looked out and smiled.

    Thee too, inspirer of the toiling swain!
Fair Autumn, yellow-robed! I'll sing of thee,
Of thy last, tempered days and sunny calms;
When all the golden Hours are on the wing,
Attending thy retreat and round thy wain,
Slow-rolling onward to the southern sky.

    Behold! the well-poised hornet hovering hangs,
With quivering pinions, in the genial blaze;
Flies off in airy circles, then returns,
And hums and dances to the beating ray:
Nor shall the man that musing walks alone,
And heedless strays within his radiant lists,
Go unchastised away. Sometimes a fleece
Of clouds, wide-scattering, with a lucid veil
Soft shadow o'er th' unruffled face of heaven;
And, through their dewy sluices, shed the sun
With tempered influence down. Then is the time
For those, whom Wisdom and whom Nature charm,
To steal themselves from the degenerate crowd,
And soar above this little scene of things:
To tread low-thoughted Vice beneath their feet,
To lay their passions in a gentle calm,
And woo lone Quiet in her silent walks.

    Now solitary, and in pensive guise,
Oft let me wander o'er the russet mead,
Or through the pining grove, where scarce is heard
One dying strain to cheer the woodman's toil:
Sad Philomel, perchance, pours forth her plaint
Far through the withering copse. Meanwhile, the leaves,
That late the forest clad with lively green,
Nipped by the drizzly night, and sallow-hued,
Fall, wavering, through the air; or shower amain,
Urged by the breeze that sobs amid the boughs.

Then list'ning hares forsake the rustling woods,
And, starting at the frequent noise, escape
To the rough stubble and the rushy fen.
Then woodcocks o'er the fluctuating main,
That glimmers to the glimpses of the moon,
Stretch their long voyage to the woodland glade,
Where, wheeling with uncertain flight, they mock
The nimble fowler's aim. Now Nature droops;
Languish the living herbs with pale decay,
And all the various family of flowers
Their sunny robes resign. The falling fruits,
Through the still night, forsake the parent-bough,
That, in the first grey glances of the dawn,
Looks wild, and wonders at the wintry waste.

   The year, yet pleasing but declining fast,
Soft o'er the secret soul, in gentle gales,
A philosophic melancholy breathes,
And bears the swelling thought aloft to heaven.
Then forming fancy rouses to conceive
What never mingled with the vulgar's dream:
Then wake the tender pang, the pitying tear,
The sigh for suffering worth, the wish preferred
For humankind, the joy to see them blessed,
And all the social offspring of the heart!

   Oh! bear me then to high, embowering shades,
To twilight groves, and visionary vales,
To weeping grottoes and to hoary caves;
Where angel-forms are seen, and voices heard,
Sighed in low whispers, that abstract the soul
From outward sense, far into worlds remote.

   Now, when the western sun withdraws the day,
And humid Evening, gliding o'er the sky,
In her chill progress checks the straggling beams,
And robs them of their gathered, vapoury prey,
Where marshes stagnate and where rivers wind,
Cluster the rolling fogs, and swim along
The dusky-mantled lawn: then slow descend,
Once more to mingle with their wat'ry friends.

The vivid stars shine out in radiant files,
And boundless ether glows; till the fair moon
Shows her broad visage in the crimsoned east;
Now, stooping, seems to kiss the passing cloud,
Now o'er the pure cerulean rides sublime.
Wide the pale deluge floats with silver waves,
O'er the skied mountain to the low-laid vale;
From the white rocks, with dim reflection, gleams,
And faintly glitters through the waving shades.

   All night, abundant dews unnoted fall,
And, at return of morning, silver o'er
The face of mother-earth; from every branch
Depending, tremble the translucent gems,
And, quivering, seem to fall away, yet cling,
And sparkle in the sun, whose rising eye,
With fogs bedimmed, portends a beauteous day.

   Now giddy youth, whom headlong passions fire,
Rouse the wild game, and stain the guiltless grove
With violence and death; yet call it sport
To scatter ruin through the realms of Love,
And Peace, that thinks no ill: but these the Muse,
Whose charity unlimited extends
As wide as Nature works, disdains to sing,
Returning to her nobler theme in view.

   For see! where Winter comes, himself confessed,
Striding the gloomy blast. First rains obscure
Drive through the mingling skies with tempest foul;
Beat on the mountain's brow, and shake the woods
That, sounding, wave below. The dreary plain
Lies overwhelmed and lost. The bellying clouds
Combine and, deepening into night, shut up
The day's fair face. The wanderers of heaven,
Each to his home, retire; save those that love
To take their pastime in the troubled air,
And, skimming, flutter round the dimply flood.
The cattle from th' untasted fields return,
And ask, with meaning low, their wonted stalls,
Or ruminate in the contiguous shade:

Thither the household, feathery people crowd,
The crested cock with all his female train,
Pensive and wet. Meanwhile, the cottage-swain
Hangs o'er th' enlivening blaze and, taleful, there
Recounts his simple frolic: much he talks
And much he laughs, nor recks the storm that blows
Without, and rattles on his humble roof.

At last the muddy deluge pours along,
Resistless, roaring; dreadful down it comes
From the chapped mountain and the mossy wild,
Tumbling through rocks abrupt, and sounding far:
Then o'er the sanded valley, floating, spreads,
Calm, sluggish, silent; till again constrained
Betwixt two meeting hills, it bursts a way,
Where rocks and woods o'erhang the turbid stream.
There gathering triple force, rapid and deep,
It boils, and wheels, and foams, and thunders through.

Nature! great parent! whose directing hand
Rolls round the seasons of the changeful year,
How mighty, how majestic are thy works!
With what a pleasing dread they swell the soul,
That sees, astonished! and astonished sings!
You too, ye winds! that now begin to blow
With boisterous sweep, I raise my voice to you.
Where are your stores, ye viewless beings! say,
Where your aerial magazines reserved,
Against the day of tempest perilous?
In what untravelled country of the air,
Hushed in still silence, sleep you when 'tis calm?

Late, in the louring sky, red, fiery streaks
Begin to flush about; the reeling clouds
Stagger with dizzy aim, as doubting yet
Which master to obey; while rising slow,
Sad, in the leaden-coloured east, the moon
Wears a bleak circle round her sullied orb.
Then issues forth the storm with loud control,
And the thin fabric of the pillared air
O'erturns at once. Prone on th' uncertain main

Descends th' ethereal force, and ploughs its waves
With dreadful rift: from the mid-deep appears,
Surge after surge, the rising, wat'ry war.
Whitening, the angry billows roll immense,
And roar their terrors through the shuddering soul
Of feeble man, amidst their fury caught,
And dashed upon his fate. Then, o'er the cliff
Where dwells the sea-mew, unconfined they fly,
And, hurrying, swallow up the sterile shore.

    The mountain growls, and all its sturdy sons
Stoop to the bottom of the rocks they shade:
Lone on its midnight-side, and all aghast,
The dark, wayfaring stranger, breathless, toils,
And climbs against the blast –
Low waves the rooted forest, vexed, and sheds
What of its leafy honours yet remains.
Thus, struggling through the dissipated grove,
The whirling tempest raves along the plain;
And, on the cottage thatched or lordly dome
Keen-fastening, shakes 'em to the solid base.
Sleep, frighted, flies; the hollow chimney howls,
The windows rattle, and the hinges creak.

    Then too, they say, through all the burthened air
Long groans are heard, shrill sounds and distant sighs,
That, murmured by the demon of the night,
Warn the devoted wretch of woe and death!
Wild uproar lords it wide: the clouds commixed
With stars, swift-gliding, sweep along the sky.
All nature reels. But hark! the Almighty speaks:
Instant the chidden storm begins to pant,
And dies at once into a noiseless calm.

    As yet 'tis midnight's reign; the weary clouds,
Slow-meeting, mingle into solid gloom.
Now, while the drowsy world lies lost in sleep,
Let me associate with the low-browed Night,
And Contemplation, her sedate compeer;
Let me shake off th' intrusive cares of day,
And lay the meddling senses all aside.

And now, ye lying Vanities of life!
You ever-tempting, ever-cheating train!
Where are you now? and what is your amount?
Vexation, disappointment and remorse.
Sad, sickening thought! and yet deluded man,
A scene of wild, disjointed visions past,
And broken slumbers, rises still resolved,
With new-flushed hopes, to run your giddy round.

Father of light and life! Thou Good Supreme,
O! teach me what is good! teach me thyself!
Save me from folly, vanity and vice,
From every low pursuit! and feed my soul
With knowledge, conscious peace and virtue pure,
Sacred, substantial, never-fading bliss!

Lo! from the livid east or piercing north,
Thick clouds ascend, in whose capacious womb
A vapoury deluge lies, to snow congealed:
Heavy, they roll their fleecy world along,
And the sky saddens with th' impending storm.
Through the hushed air the whitening shower descends,
At first thin-wavering; till at last the flakes
Fall broad and wide and fast, dimming the day
With a continual flow. See! sudden hoared,
The woods beneath the stainless burden bow;
Black'ning, along the mazy stream it melts.
Earth's universal face, deep-hid and chill,
Is all one dazzling waste. The labourer-ox
Stands covered o'er with snow, and then demands
The fruit of all his toil. The fowls of heaven,
Tamed by the cruel season, crowd around
The winnowing store, and claim the little boon
That Providence allows. The foodless wilds
Pour forth their brown inhabitants; the hare,
Though timorous of heart, and hard beset
By death in various forms, dark snares, and dogs,
And more unpitying men, the garden seeks,
Urged on by fearless want. The bleating kind
Eye the bleak heavens, and next the glistening earth,

With looks of dumb despair; then sad, dispersed,
Dig for the withered herb through heaps of snow.

Now, shepherds, to your helpless charge be kind;
Baffle the raging year, and fill their pens
With food at will; lodge them below the blast,
And watch them strict: for from the bellowing east,
In this dire season, oft the whirlwind's wing
Sweeps up the burthen of whole wintry plains
In one fierce blast, and o'er th' unhappy flocks,
Lodged in the hollow of two neighbouring hills,
The billowy tempest whelms; till, upwards urged,
The valley to a shining mountain swells,
That curls its wreaths amid the freezing sky.

Now, amid all the rigours of the year,
In the wild depth of winter, while without
The ceaseless winds blow keen, be my retreat
A rural, sheltered, solitary scene,
Where ruddy fire and beaming tapers join
To chase the cheerless gloom: there let me sit,
And hold high converse with the mighty dead,
Sages of ancient times, as gods revered,
As gods beneficent, who blessed mankind
With arts and arms, and humanized a world.
Roused at th' inspiring thought, I throw aside
The long-lived volume and, deep-musing, hail
The sacred shades that, slowly-rising, pass
Before my wondering eyes. First, Socrates,
Truth's early champion, martyr for his god;
Solon the next, who built his commonweal
On equity's firm base; Lycurgus then,
Severely good; and him of rugged Rome,
Numa, who softened her rapacious sons;
Cimon sweet-souled, and Aristides just;
Unconquered Cato, virtuous in extreme;
With that attempered hero, mild and firm,
Who wept the brother, while the tyrant bled;
Scipio, the humane warrior, gently brave,
Fair learning's friend, who early sought the shade,

To dwell with Innocence and Truth retired;
And, equal to the best, the Theban, he
Who, single, raised his country into fame.
Thousands behind, the boast of Greece and Rome,
Whom Virtue owns, the tribute of a verse
Demand, but who can count the stars of heaven?
Who sing their influence on this lower world?
But see who yonder comes! nor comes alone,
With sober state and of majestic mien,
The Sister-Muses in his train. 'Tis he!
Maro! the best of poets and of men!
Great Homer too appears, of daring wing!
Parent of song! and, equal, by his side,
The British Muse; joined hand in hand they walk,
Darkling, nor miss their way to fame's ascent.

    Society divine! Immortal minds!
Still visit thus my nights, for you reserved,
And mount my soaring soul to deeds like yours.
Silence! thou lonely power! the door be thine:
See on the hallowed hour that none intrude,
Save Lycidas, the friend with sense refined,
Learning digested well, exalted faith,
Unstudied wit, and humour ever gay.

    Clear frost succeeds and, through the blue serene,
For sight too fine, th' ethereal nitre flies,
To bake the glebe and bind the slipp'ry flood.
This of the wintry season is the prime;
Pure are the days, and lustrous are the nights,
Brightened with starry worlds till then unseen.
Meanwhile the orient, darkly red, breathes forth
An icy gale that, in its mid-career,
Arrests the bickering stream. The nightly sky,
And all her glowing constellations, pour
Their rigid influence down. It freezes on
Till morn, late-rising, o'er the drooping world
Lifts her pale eye, unjoyous: then appears
The various labour of the silent night,
The pendant icicle, the frost-work fair

Where thousand figures rise, the crusted snow,
Though white, made whiter by the fining north.
On blithesome frolics bent, the youthful swains,
While every work of man is laid at rest,
Rush o'er the wat'ry plains and, shuddering, view
The fearful deeps below; or with the gun
And faithful spaniel range the ravaged fields,
And, adding to the ruins of the year,
Distress the feathery or the footed game.

    But hark! the nightly winds, with hollow voice,
Blow blustering from the south. The frost subdued
Gradual resolves into a weeping thaw.
Spotted, the mountains shine; loose sleet descends,
And floods the country round; the rivers swell,
Impatient for the day. Those sullen seas,
That wash th' ungenial pole, will rest no more
Beneath the shackles of the mighty north,
But, rousing all their waves, resistless heave.
And hark! the length'ning roar continuous runs
Athwart the rifted main; at once it bursts,
And piles a thousand mountains to the clouds!
Ill fares the bark, the wretches' last resort,
That, lost amid the floating fragments, moors
Beneath the shelter of an icy isle,
While night o'erwhelms the sea, and horror looks
More horrible. Can human hearts endure
Th' assembled mischiefs that besiege them round:
Unlist'ning hunger, fainting weariness,
The roar of winds and waves, the crush of ice,
Now ceasing, now renewed with louder rage,
And bellowing round the main? Nations remote,
Shook from their midnight-slumbers, deem they hear
Portentous thunder in the troubled sky.
More to embroil the deep, leviathan
And his unwieldy train, in horrid sport,
Tempest the loosened brine; while through the gloom,
Far from the dire, unhospitable shore,
The lion's rage, the wolf's sad howl is heard,

And all the fell society of night.
Yet Providence, that ever-waking eye,
Looks down with pity on the fruitless toil
Of mortals lost to hope, and lights them safe
Through all this dreary labyrinth of fate.

    'Tis done! Dread Winter has subdued the year,
And reigns tremendous o'er the desert plains!
How dead the vegetable kingdom lies!
How dumb the tuneful! Horror wide extends
His solitary empire. Now, fond Man!
Behold thy pictured life: pass some few years,
Thy flow'ring Spring, thy shortlived Summer's strength,
Thy sober Autumn fading into age,
And pale, concluding Winter shuts thy scene,
And shrouds thee in the grave. Where now are fled
Those dreams of greatness? those unsolid hopes
Of happiness? those longings after fame?
Those restless cares? those busy, bustling days?
Those nights of secret guilt? those veering thoughts,
Flutt'ring 'twixt good and ill, that shared thy life?
All now are vanished! Virtue sole survives,
Immortal, mankind's never-failing friend,
His guide to happiness on high. And see!
'Tis come, the glorious Morn! the second birth
Of heaven and earth! awakening Nature hears
Th' almighty trumpet's voice, and starts to life,
Renewed, unfading. Now th' eternal Scheme,
That dark perplexity, that mystic maze,
Which sight could never trace, nor heart conceive,
To Reason's eye refined, clears up apace.
Angels and men, astonished, pause – and dread
To travel through the depths of Providence,
Untried, unbounded. Ye vain learned! see,
And, prostrate in the dust, adore that Power
And Goodness, oft arraigned. See now the cause,
Why conscious worth, oppressed, in secret long
Mourned, unregarded; why the good man's share
In life was gall and bitterness of soul;

Why the lone widow and her orphans pined,
In starving solitude; while Luxury,
In palaces, lay prompting her low thought
To form unreal wants; why heaven-born Faith
And Charity, prime grace! wore the red marks
Of Persecution's scourge; why licensed Pain,
That cruel spoiler, that embosomed foe,
Imbittered all our bliss. Ye good distressed!
Ye noble few! that here unbending stand
Beneath life's pressures, yet a little while,
And all your woes are past. Time swiftly fleets,
And wished Eternity, approaching, brings
Life undecaying, love without allay,
Pure, flowing joy, and happiness sincere.

JAMES THOMSON

Peter Grimes; the Outcast

Thus by himself compelled to live each day,
To wait for certain hours the tide's delay;
At the same times the same dull views to see,
The bounding marsh-bank and the blighted tree;
The water only, when the tides were high,
When low, the mud half-covered and half-dry;
The sun-burnt tar that blisters on the planks,
And bank-side stakes in their uneven ranks;
Heaps of entangled weeds that slowly float,
As the tide rolls by the impeded boat.

   When tides were neap, and, in the sultry day,
Through the tall bounding mud-banks made their way,
Which on each side rose swelling, and below
The dark warm flood ran silently and slow;
There anchoring, Peter chose from man to hide,
There hang his head, and view the lazy tide
In the hot slimy channel slowly glide;
Where the small eels that left the deeper way

For the warm shore, within the shallows play;
Where gaping mussels, left upon the mud,
Slope their slow passage to the fallen flood; –
Here dull and hopeless he'd lie down and trace
How sidelong crabs had scrawled their crooked race;
Or sadly listern to the tuneless cry
Of fishing gull or clanging golden-eye;
What time the sea-birds to the marsh would come,
And the loud bittern, from the bull-rush home,
Gave from the salt-ditch side the bellowing boom:
He nursed the feelings these dull scenes produce,
And loved to stop beside the opening sluice;
Where the small stream, confined in narrow bound,
Ran with a dull, unvaried, saddening sound;
Where all, presented to the eye or ear,
Oppressed the soul with misery, grief, and fear.

GEORGE CRABBE

PENGUIN POPULAR CLASSICS

Published or forthcoming

PENGUIN POPULAR CLASSICS

Published or forthcoming

PENGUIN POPULAR CLASSICS

Published or forthcoming